C

Effective Mooring

Your Guide to Mooring Equipment and Operations

3rd Edition

The OCIMF mission is to be the foremost authority on the safe and environmentally responsible operation of oil tankers, terminals and offshore support vessels, promoting continuous improvement in standards of design and operation.

©Copyright OCIMF 2010

Issued by the
Oil Companies International Marine Forum
29 Queen Anns Gate
London
SW1H 9BU
United Kingdom

First published 1989
Second Edition 2005
Third Edition 2010
Reprinted 2012

ISBN: 978 1 905331 65 9

© Oil Companies International Marine Forum, Bermuda

British Library Cataloguing in Publication Data
A catalogue record for this book is available from the British Library.

The Oil Companies International Marine Forum (OCIMF)

is a voluntary association of oil companies having an interest in the shipment and terminalling of crude oil and oil products. OCIMF is organised to represent its membership before, and to consult with, the International Maritime Organization and other governmental bodies on matters relating to the shipment and terminalling of crude oil and oil products, including marine pollution and safety.

Terms of Use

The advice and information given in this 'Effective Mooring' ('Guide') is intended purely as guidance to be used at the user's own risk. Acceptance or otherwise of recommendations and/or guidance in this Guide is entirely voluntary. The use of the terms 'will', 'shall', 'must' and other similar such words, are for convenience only, and nothing in this Guide is intended or should be construed as establishing standards or requirements. No warranties or representations are given nor is any duty of care or responsibility accepted by the Oil Companies International Marine Forum (OCIMF), the membership or employees of OCIMF or by any person, firm, corporation or organisation (who or which has been in any way concerned with the furnishing of information or data, the compilation or any translation, publishing, supply or sale of the Guide) for the accuracy of any information or advice given in the Guide or any omission from the Guide or for any consequence whatsoever resulting directly or indirectly from compliance with, adoption of or reliance on guidance contained in the Guide even if caused by a failure to exercise reasonable care on the part of any of the aforementioned parties.

Witherby Seamanship International is a division of Witherby Publishing Group Ltd

Published by

Witherby Publishing Group Ltd
4 Dunlop Square, Livingston,
Edinburgh, EH54 8SB,
Scotland, UK

Tel No: +44(0)1506 463 227
Fax No: +44(0)1506 468 999
Email: info@emailws.com
Web: www.witherbys.com

Printed and bound in Great Britain by Bell & Bain Ltd, Glasgow

©Copyright OCIMF 2010

Introduction

The aim of this guide is to complement existing technical publications and rules and regulations with one that is deliberately written in a style that communicates effectively with seafarers at all levels.

The emphasis is on SAFETY. Its intention is to make shipboard staff more aware of the hazards associated with mooring equipment and mooring operations by providing a better understanding of the subject. A summary of the personal safety items mentioned throughout the text is given in Chapter 7.

This guide is designed to be self-contained. However, readers who are interested in obtaining more detailed technical information should refer to other OCIMF documents dealing with mooring, in particular *Mooring Equipment Guidelines*.

Although this guide has been written primarily with oil and gas tankers in mind, most of its contents apply equally to other types of vessels.

This guide is derived from one entitled 'Effective Mooring' that was originally published by Shell International Marine in 1976. Experience over the last 30 years has shown that 'Effective Mooring' has been successful in putting across its message and so, therefore, the same general format is retained in this revision.

This 2010 revision brings the whole topic up-to-date by referencing information contained within the 3rd edition of OCIMF *Mooring Equipment Guidelines,* published in 2008. Also included is guidance on mooring contained in other OCIMF publications that address, for example, tandem mooring, operations at single and multi-buoy moorings and ship-to-ship transfers.

Finally, it is stressed that this guide is not a book of rules. It contains recommendations on safety, minimum equipment levels and good operating practices, but it must always be remembered that if more stringent international, national or local regulations apply, they must take precedence.

OCIMF always welcome suggestions for improvements that can be considered for inclusion in future editions. Comments may be forwarded to OCIMF at the following address:

Oil Companies International Marine Forum
29 Queen Anne's Gate
London SW1H 9BU
England

Telephone: +44 (0)20 7654 1200
Email: enquiries@ocimf.com

Contents

Introduction iii

Section 1
Effective Mooring 1
1.1 What Does a Mooring System Do? 3
1.2 How Big are these Forces? 4
1.3 Mooring Layout 7
1.4 Wires or Synthetic Fibre Ropes 9
1.5 Elasticity 10
1.6 Vertical Angle (Dip) 13
1.7 Mixed Moorings 13
1.8 Synthetic Fibre Tails 13
1.9 Marine Loading Arms 15
1.10 Quick Release Hooks 16

Section 2
Mooring Winches 17
2.1 Winch Control Types 19
2.2 Winch Drums 21
2.3 Winch Brakes 21
2.4 Correct Layering 22
2.5 Split Drum Winches 23
2.6 Undivided Drum Winches 24
2.7 Correct Reeling 24
2.8 Brake Condition 25
2.9 Testing Brakes 26
2.10 Application of Brake 26
2.11 Incorrect Use of Brake 28
2.12 Exceptional Circumstances 28
2.13 Winch in Gear 29
2.14 Freezing Weather 29
2.15 Joining a New Ship 30
2.16 Safety Reminders 31

Section 3
Wire Mooring Lines 33
3.1 Construction of Wire Mooring Lines 35
3.2 Definitions 36
3.3 Typical Steel Wire Rope Constructions 37
3.4 Bend Radius 38
3.5 Advantages of Steel Wire Ropes 39
3.6 Certification 40
3.7 Stoppers for Use with Steel Wires 40
3.8 Care of Wire 43
3.9 Maintenance of Steel Wire Mooring Ropes 44
3.10 Selection of Anchor Point for 1st Layer of Wire on a Drum 45
3.11 Splicing Wire 47
3.12 Safety Reminders 48

Section 4
Synthetic Fibre Ropes 49
4.1 Construction of Synthetic Fibre Ropes 51
4.2 Types of Material Used 53
4.3 Relative Minimum Breaking Loads of Synthetic Ropes 55
4.4 Certification 55
4.5 Stoppers for Use with Synthetic Ropes 55
4.6 Belaying Synthetic Fibre Ropes on Bitts 56
4.7 Snap Back 57
4.8 Rope Care 59
4.9 Rope Inspection 60
4.10 Splicing 60
4.11 Safety Reminders 61

Section 5
Offshore Operations 63
5.1 Multi-Buoy Moorings 65
5.2 Single Point Moorings 69
5.3 Mooring to FPSOs and FSOs 72
5.4 Dedicated Shuttle Tankers 73
5.5 Conventional Tankers 74
5.6 Mooring Operation 75
5.7 Ship-to-Ship Transfer (STS) 76

Section 6
Windlasses and Anchoring 81

6.1 Brakes 84
6.2 Cable Stoppers 84
6.3 Anchor Cables 85
6.4 Communication 85
6.5 Maintenance of Windlass Brakes 86
6.6 Adjustments 86
6.7 Prolonged Periods of Non-Use 87
6.8 Safety Reminders 87

Section 7
Personal Safety 89

7.1 Handling of Moorings 91
7.2 Safe Handling of Tug Lines 93
7.3 Gloves 95
7.4 Safety Reminders 96

Effective Mooring,
Your Guide to Mooring Equipment and Operations

Effective Mooring

Section 1

Effective Mooring

Section 1 *Effective Mooring*

Effective Mooring

1.1 What Does a Mooring System Do?

A mooring system prevents the ship from drifting away from a berth and holds the ship in place in relation to the loading/discharging arms or hoses, which may only have limited freedom of movement. Mooring lines may also assist in heaving the ship alongside a berth and can be used to assist in unberthing.

The mooring system has to maintain the ship's position against forces that will be trying to move it. These may be caused by one or more of the following:

- Wind
- current
- tides
- surge due to passing ships
- waves and swell
- change of draft, trim and list
- ice.

Effective Mooring

1.2 How Big are these Forces?

At a well sited berth, the greatest forces arise from wind and current, but to design a mooring system capable of resisting the extreme conditions of wind and current would create problems in both the size and cost of equipment. It is, therefore, normal practice to establish arbitrary wind and current criteria and then design the mooring system to meet these criteria.

Commonly used criteria are:

- Wind 60 knots from any direction, plus a current on the beam of 0.75 knots, or
- wind 60 knots from any direction, plus a current from ahead or astern of 3 knots.

Both wind and current forces are proportional to the square of the wind or current speed, thus the force caused by a sustained 60 knot wind is 4 times that caused by a 30 knot wind, and the force exerted by a 3 knot current is 9 times that exerted by a 1 knot current.

Wind speed increases with height above sea level. For example, a wind of 60 knots at 10 metres will be more than 75 knots at 30 metres, but only 30 knots at 2 metres (just above man-high). So that information from different sites can be compared, it is usual to correct all anemometer readings to an equivalent height of 10 metres.

Because of the speed/force and speed/height characteristics of wind behaviour, freeboard is a major and sometimes critical factor for safe mooring.

In the case of currents, forces become significant when the clearance under the keel is small in relation to the draft. In this situation, and when the current is from the beam, the ship begins to act as a major obstruction to a current, which must either escape around the bow or stern or accelerate under the keel. A similar but less pronounced effect occurs with currents aligned to the ship's fore and aft axis.

Section 1 Effective Mooring

A well designed berth will be sited so that the current will be end on or nearly end on, but Figure 1 shows how the current force due to a beam current increases as the 'depth/draft ratio' is reduced.

12 tonnes	25 tonnes	40 tonnes	70 tonnes
118 kN	245 kN	392 kN	686 kN
5 × Draft or more	1.6 × Draft	0.5 × Draft	0.2 × Draft

Assumes 2 knot current, 5° off the bow

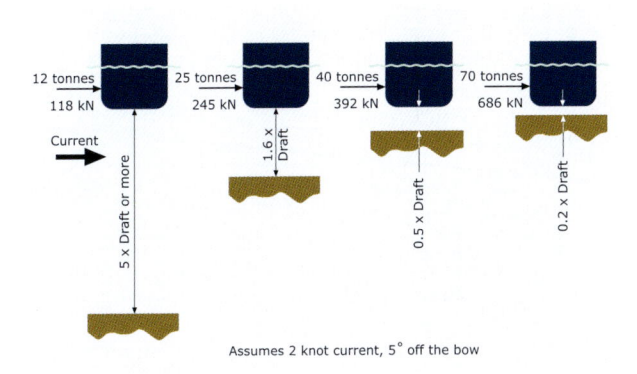

Fig. 1 Effect of Underkeel Clearance on Current Force

Ballasting the ship down will usually reduce the total forces acting on a ship as the wind gradient effect is greater than the underkeel clearance effect.

Effective Mooring

The following table provides some examples of the forces on various conventional ship sizes due to wind (60 knots) and current (3 knots ahead or 0.75 knots abeam).

Summer dwt		Transverse Forces tonnes		Longitudinal Forces tonnes	
		Wind	Current	Wind	Current
18,000	Loaded	33	16	17	6
	Ballast	84	9	21	4
30,000	Loaded	50	42	23	16
	Ballast	112	21	26	9
70,000	Loaded	67	78	25	30
	Ballast	168	21	34	18
150,000	Loaded	98	107	34	42
	Ballast	213	29	46	23
300,000	Loaded	156	171	51	67
	Ballast	336	48	72	25
LNG Carrier	125,000 m^3	396	76	78	30

A ship moves up and down alongside a berth through the actions of both the tide and cargo operations. It is perhaps stating the obvious that, as a ship rises or falls, the tensions in the mooring lines will change. As they tighten the ship will tend to move in towards the berth; conversely, as the height above the jetty decreases, the lines will become slack and the ship is likely to move away from her proper position.

Regular line tending is the only remedy for managing movement in the berth while the ship is moored.

Forces caused by passing ships, waves or swell are complex and continually varying, although at most berths they will not create problems for the ship that is using her equipment properly.

Section 1 *Effective Mooring*

Where these forces are unusually large, jetty operators should have made some provision to supplement the ship's system. Attention to mooring restraint is particularly important in the case of a deep draft loaded ship with minimum underkeel clearance and berthed close to a shipping lane. The force from passing ships, in this situation, could be large enough to part the lines or pull the ship off the dock if the lines were slack.

1.3 Mooring Layout

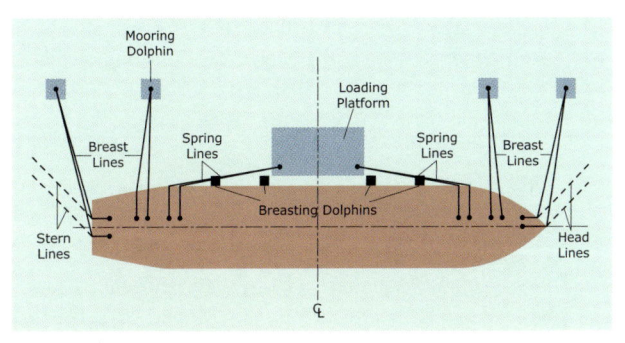

Fig. 2 Typical Mooring Arrangement

Effective Mooring

While it is often difficult in practice to achieve an ideal mooring layout, Figure 2 shows a typical mooring arrangement designed to resist environmental forces acting on the ship.

These forces, particularly wind, can come from any direction, but when discussing mooring systems the forces are split into longitudinal and transverse components. A ship's equipment can always be employed to the best advantage if the following general principles are remembered:

- Breast lines provide the bulk of the transverse restraint against off-the-berth forces
- spring lines provide the largest proportion of the longitudinal restraint. It should be noted that spring lines provide restraint in two directions, forward and aft, but that only one set of springs will be stressed at any one time
- very short lengths of line should be avoided when possible, as such lines will take a greater proportion of the total load when movement of the ship occurs. Short lines are also the ones most seriously affected by 'dip' (see page 13, Figure 6).

Although head lines and stern lines, because of their direction, have the effect of providing some restraint against both longitudinal and transverse forces, they actually contribute less to the overall mooring strength than is commonly assumed.

Head and stern lines contribute less to overall mooring strength because the direction of the largest forces encountered is usually either nearly transverse or nearly longitudinal, i.e. along the lines of action of breast or spring lines respectively.

The most extreme conditions, i.e. light ship and combined beam wind and current, will usually produce a resultant force vector within about 25 degrees off the beam.

In the example illustrated in Figure 3, with the head lines leading at 45 degrees to the breast lines, the contribution of the head lines to the total transverse restraint is only about 26% of the

Section 1 *Effective Mooring*

whole. Even if the total resultant force aligns with a head line, the line takes only 41% of the load with the breast line and spring line sharing the remaining 59%.

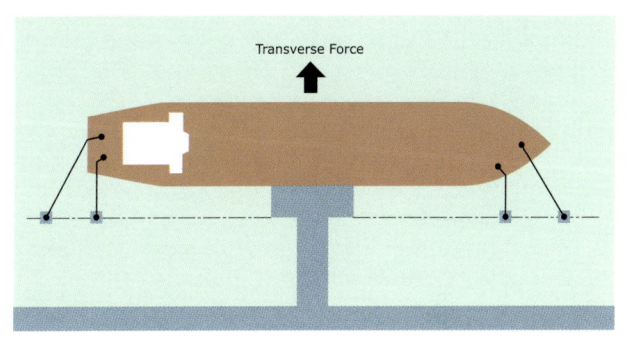

Fig. 3 Transverse Force

1.4 Wires or Synthetic Fibre Ropes

The key factors for any wire or rope are strength, usually described by reference to Minimum Breaking Load (MBL), and elasticity, a measure of its stretch under load.

Conventional synthetic fibre ropes are adequately strong and of a reasonable size for mooring small to medium sized ships, but for larger sizes of ships the ropes may become too large to handle unless fitted on self stowing winches. Further, the handling of a large number of such ropes would be difficult.

In addition, most synthetic fibre ropes stretch far more than wires. A typical figure for the extension of a polyamide rope at 70% of MBL is around 20% compared with less than 2% for a wire (see Figure 4). As the mooring ropes of a VLCC may reach 70 to 100 metres, it is clear that a mooring system comprising of conventional synthetic fibre ropes is unlikely to provide the accurate positioning demanded by the loading arms.

While smaller ships may be equipped with conventional synthetic fibre ropes, it is normal for larger ships to be equipped

Effective Mooring

with wires fitted to self-stowing winches. Even on smaller ships, wires, if fitted, are normally on self-stowing winches for ease and safety of handling. On new buildings it is common practice for the synthetic ropes to be fitted to self-stowing winches.

A synthetic fibre rope fitted to a self-stowing winch is sometimes provided at each end of the ship. Its purpose is to act as the 'first line ashore' as its light weight and buoyancy make for easy handling in a mooring boat, on the jetty, and on board. It can, therefore, be sent ashore easily when the ship is some distance from the berth and then used to assist in heaving the ship alongside the berth. However, because of its greater elasticity, it should not be considered as part of the actual mooring system unless the other head and stern lines are of a similar material.

With the ready availability of high modulus synthetic fibre ropes, such as those made from aramid and high modulus polyethylene (HMPE) fibres, it is becoming more common for larger vessels to be fitted with mooring outfits comprised of these materials. The initial cost is higher than a conventional wire mooring outfit but benefits can be realised from ease of handling and associated shorter mooring times, less maintenance costs and, where pennants are used, joining shackles are not always required.

1.5 Elasticity

The elasticity of mooring lines is important because it determines how the total load will be shared between a number of lines.

If two lines of the same size and material are run out in the same direction and pre-tensioned, but one is secured to a hook twice as far away as the other, the shorter line will take two thirds of any additional imposed load, the longer line will take only one third.

Section 1 *Effective Mooring*

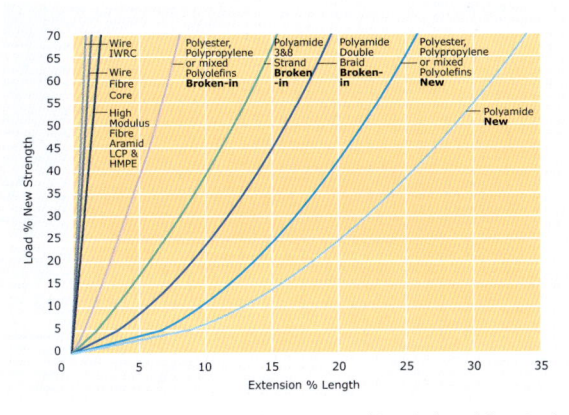

Fig. 4 Load-Extension Characteristics of Mooring Lines (Note: 'polyamide' previously referred to as 'nylon')

Therefore, two or more lines leading in the same direction should, as far as possible, be of the same length.

If two lines are the same length, the same breaking strength and have the same lead, but one is a wire of 1.5% full load extension and the other is a conventional synthetic line of 30% full load extension, the wire will take 95% of the extra load, the synthetic only 5%.

Therefore, two or more lines leading in the same direction should always be of the same material. Never mix wire and conventional synthetic fibre lines leading in the same direction if it can be avoided.

For further discussion on elasticity including load-extension characteristics, refer to *Mooring Equipment Guidelines*.

11

©Copyright OCIMF 2010

Effective Mooring

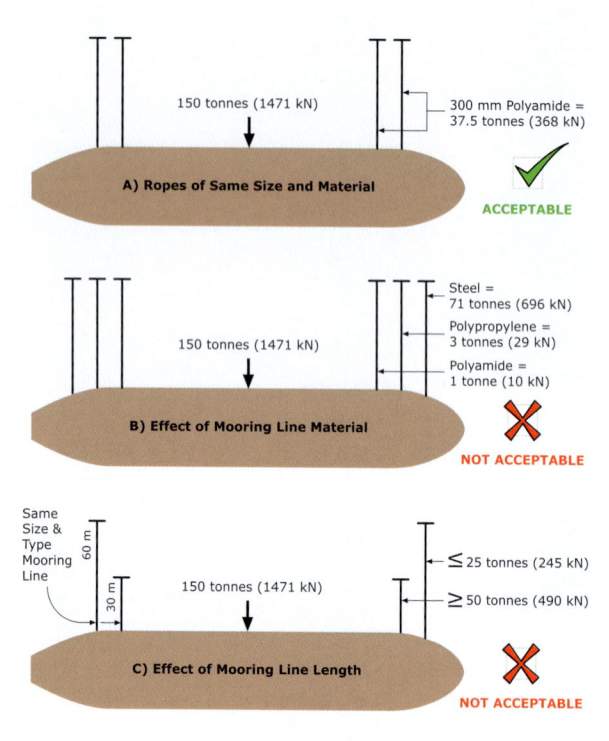

A) Ropes of Same Size and Material
150 tonnes (1471 kN)
300 mm Polyamide = 37.5 tonnes (368 kN)
✓ ACCEPTABLE

B) Effect of Mooring Line Material
150 tonnes (1471 kN)
Steel = 71 tonnes (696 kN)
Polypropylene = 3 tonnes (29 kN)
Polyamide = 1 tonne (10 kN)
✗ NOT ACCEPTABLE

C) Effect of Mooring Line Length
Same Size & Type Mooring Line
60 m
30 m
150 tonnes (1471 kN)
≤ 25 tonnes (245 kN)
≥ 50 tonnes (490 kN)
✗ NOT ACCEPTABLE

Note: All Loads Are Approximate

Fig. 5 Effect of Mooring Elasticity on Restraint Capability

Elasticity of a given type of rope also varies with its diameter or circumference, larger ropes extending less than smaller ropes. Although this is unlikely to be an important factor as mooring lines on a ship are usually of uniform diameter or circumference, it should be borne in mind when ordering new lines.

Section 1 *Effective Mooring*

1.6 **Vertical Angle (Dip)**

Whenever a line is unable to act in exactly the same direction as the force it is trying to withstand, its holding power is reduced. Therefore, a short line to a mooring hook substantially lower than the ship's fairlead will be of limited value. The effectiveness is proportional to the cosine of the angle the line makes to the horizontal, i.e. for 30 degrees the line is 87% effective, for 45 degrees 71 % effective (Figure 6). It is recommended, where possible, that this vertical angle, or dip, be less than 25 degrees.

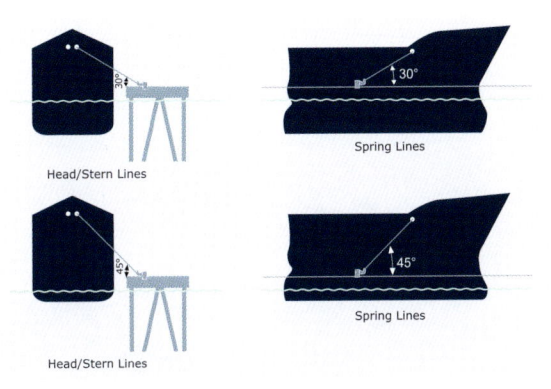

Fig. 6 Vertical Angle (Dip)

1.7 **Mixed Moorings**

Preferably, a ship's mooring lines should all be of similar material and contruction, but not every ship is fortunate enough to possess an all-wire or all-synthetic mooring outfit. In such cases, the best must be made of a mixture of wires and conventional synthetic fibre ropes. Wherever possible in these cases, use the wires for the spring and breast lines and the conventional synthetic ropes for headlines and stern lines.

1.8 **Synthetic Fibre Tails**

Although moorings with low elasticity (such as wires or high modulus synthetic fibre ropes) provide the most effective

13

©Copyright OCIMF 2010

Effective Mooring

mooring system, that same low elasticity can also pose its own problems, particularly at berths where sea and swell, or perhaps passing ships, can impart shock (dynamic) loadings to the mooring system. In such cases, there may be insufficient elasticity to prevent failure of the mooring lines.

This problem can be overcome by introducing a degree of elasticity by attaching synthetic fibre tails to the end of the lines. With wires, these are attached by means of special joining shackles designed to minimise wear on the wire (see Figure 7). Ordinary 'D' or 'bow' shackles should not be used as these will quickly damage both wire and tail. When attaching a synthetic fibre tail to a high modulus rope, a joining shackle is not usually required, although manufacturer's instructions should always be followed.

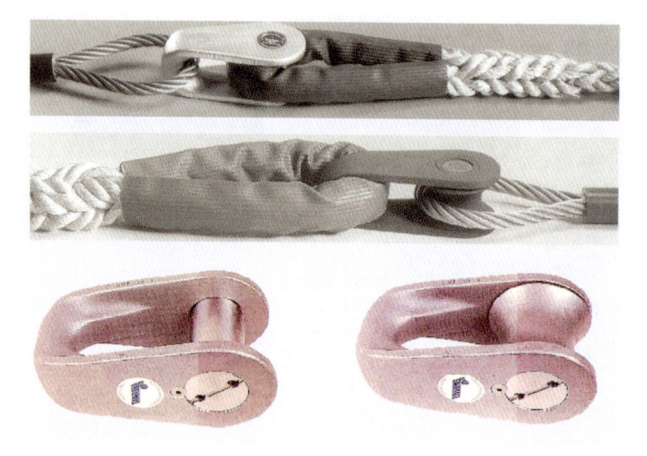

Fig. 7 Typical Links for Connecting Lines with Tails

A tail length of 11 metres provides adequate additional elasticity for sheltered pierside moorings. This is the traditional length of tail carried. However, at exposed moorings, where significant ship motions occur, a longer tail length may be necessary and some exposed terminals may require tails of up to 22 metres in length.

Section 1 *Effective Mooring*

Synthetic fibre tails are likely to deteriorate more rapidly than wire. They should, as a result, be at least 25% stronger than the lines to which they are attached. For polyamide (previously referred to as 'nylon'), they should be 37% stronger to take account of the loss of strength when wet. They should be inspected frequently or replaced at regular intervals.

The eyes of the tails should be covered in a suitable sheath to protect them from chafing. The use of leather is not recommended. Leather on immersion in salt water becomes very hard, particularly in the area around the stitching. Chaffing of synthetic fibre rope material can occur.

When tails are used on wires, the shackle may cause increased wear on the eye of the wire. This area should be inspected at regular intervals. Reference should be made to the joining shackle manufacturer's instructions with regard to the correct operation and position of the shackle.

1.9 Marine Loading Arms

The objective of good line tending is to ensure that all lines share the load to the maximum extent possible and to limit the ship's movement off, or alongside, the berth. This is of particular importance when alongside a berth equipped with marine loading arms as there is an additional requirement to keep the vessel's manifold within the operating envelope of the arms.

Among the factors taken into account in the operating envelope are the limited changes in horizontal position due to vessel drift (movement off the berth) and ranging (movement up and down the berth). There should be either a visual indication of the operating envelope and/or a system of alarms to indicate excessive range and drift.

Effective Mooring

1.10 Quick Release Hooks

Many terminals are fitted with Quick Release Hooks on the dolphins and jetties. These allow for moorings to be slipped quickly and by a minimum number of personnel. The hooks should have a SWL not less than the MBL of the largest line anticipated to be attached. They should be supplemented by capstans or winches and fairleads to facilitate the handling of ship's moorings.

> Remember, the mooring integrity of a ship alongside is not something that happens of its own accord. It needs good knowledge and use of the ship's equipment, an awareness of good mooring principles and careful planning.
>
> **Managing mooring integrity does not end when the ship is finally moored, but continues the whole time the ship is alongside.**

OCIMF

Effective Mooring,
Your Guide to Mooring Equipment and Operations

Mooring Winches

Section 2

Section 2 *Mooring Winches*

Mooring Winches

Mooring winches can be categorised by their control type (automatic or manual tensioning), drive type (hydraulic, electric or steam), by the number of drums associated with each drive (single, double or triple), by the type of drums (split or undivided) and by brake type (band or disc) and method of brake application (mechanical screw or spring-applied). Each type has it own operational characteristics and precautions. It is important that personnel operating winches are familiar with the different characteristics and have been trained in their operation.

It should be noted that a winch's heaving, or pulling, power is always less than the render force. Render force is that force required to turn the winch drum in the direction opposite its recover (heave in) direction. When a winch renders, some line will payout from the winch drum. Refer to section 2.12.

2.1 Winch Control Types

Some ships are equipped with self-tensioning winches with the intention of eliminating the need for line tending. These

Effective Mooring

are designed so that a specified line tension can be pre-set. The winch will render (pay out) when tension in the line exceeds this value and will recover (heave in) when it is less than this value.

However, experience has shown that the use of such winches while the ship is alongside is not a safe practice because the winch restraint is limited to its render load. This is small compared to what it can hold on the brake. It is possible for the winches at opposite ends of the ship to work against each other when an external force, caused by either wind or current or both, is applied to one end so that the ship could 'walk' along the jetty. In the simple illustration given in Figure 8, a ship is shown moored by one line at each end.

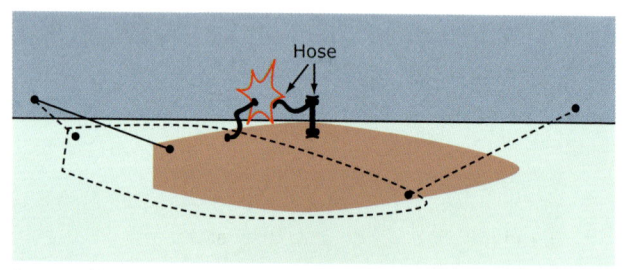

Fig. 8 Possible Effect of Winch Operating in Self-Tensioning Mode

Should the bow winch render a little for any reason (i.e. a change in direction of force of wind or current) some rope will pay out. The ship will move astern a little and the after mooring will slacken. The aft winch will heave in the slack and re-tension the line. If the disturbance is repeated or continuous, the ship will be moved progressively astern.

Mooring winches should not be left in automatic self-tensioning mode once the ship is secured alongside. On completion of mooring, the winch should be left with the brake on and out of gear.

Section 2 *Mooring Winches*

2.2 **Winch Drums**

Winch drums may be either split or undivided.

The split drum is comprised of a tension section and a line storage section. On heaving in, the mooring line is transferred from the storage section to the tension section to provide a sufficient number of turns on the tension section to hold the tension of the line on that section only and to provide sufficient extra turns to allow for line tending.

When using split drum winches, the following should be borne in mind:

- Manhandling the line from storage drum to the tension drum may be difficult and requires care and sufficient personnel
- regular attention should be paid to ensure that the appropriate number of turns is maintained on the tension drum throughout the time the ship is alongside. No more than one layer of line should be maintained on the tension drum when the line is under load.

The advantage of the split drum is that it can maintain a constant brake holding capacity and heaving force as the mooring line is always run off the first layer of the tension drum.

The undivided drum has the advantage that it avoids the need to manhandle the mooring line from section to section, as may be required with the split drum. However, it is more difficult to correctly spool and stow the mooring line on the undivided drum and, as a result, the mooring line may be damaged when tension is applied.

2.3 **Winch Brakes**

The holding capacity of winch brakes varies from ship to ship, but brakes should always be set to render at 60% of the minimum breaking load (MBL) of the mooring line to permit slippage before the line breaks.

Effective Mooring

As brakes may deteriorate in service, they should be designed to hold 80% of the line's MBL, but have the capability to be adjusted down to 60% in service.

The value of the brake holding capacity in relation to the size of line is important. There would be little point in a mooring system where lines part at loads less than the brake holding capacity. This factor should be considered when renewing lines.

Brake holding capacity is dependent upon several factors, some of which are discussed below.

2.4 *Correct Layering*

The number of layers of line on the drum affects the brake holding capacity.

The force at which the brake will render will vary dependent upon the number of layers of line left on the drum. The more layers of line on the drum the greater will be the reduction of brake holding capacity. This is illustrated in Figure 9.

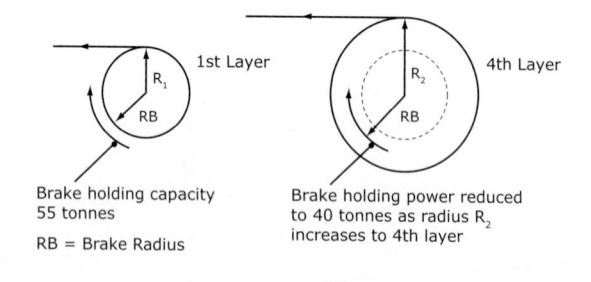

1st Layer — R_1, RB
Brake holding capacity 55 tonnes
RB = Brake Radius

4th Layer — R_2, RB
Brake holding power reduced to 40 tonnes as radius R_2 increases to 4th layer

Fig. 9 Impact of Increased Layers on Brake Holding Capacity

2.5 Split Drum Winches

The rated brake holding capacity for these winches is always quoted for only a single layer of line on the tension drum. Operation with additional layers on the tension section will decrease the brake holding capacity. This is illustrated in the following table which, as an example, shows the theoretical reduction in holding capacity for more than one layer on a 610 mm (24 inch) drum, assuming a rated brake holding capacity of 55 tonnes:

Layer of Line	Theoretical Holding Capacity	% Rated Holding Capacity
1st	55 tonnes	100%
2nd	49 tonnes	89%
3rd	45 tonnes	82%
4th	41 tonnes	75%
5th	38 tonnes	69%

The transfer section between storage and tension drums should be regularly checked to ensure that there are no chafing surfaces, especially when using synthetic fibre ropes.

Fig. 10 Typical Split Drum Winch

Effective Mooring

free there will be a loss of brake holding power and the winch operator could be under the impression that the brake is fully applied when, in fact, it may not be. Severe stresses could also be imposed on mechanical parts of the brake.

Before the end of a sea passage, during which the brakes will have been exposed to the air and sea, it is essential to check them and ensure that all control and operating handles are oiled or greased and are free and easy to use, that all linkages are greased, and that the brake drums and linings are clean and (as far as possible) dry.

2.9 Testing Brakes

Deterioration of the brake holding capacity will be caused by normal wearing down of the brake linings. Therefore, brake holding capacity should be tested annually, after completion of any modification or repair involving the brake, or upon any evidence of premature brake slippage or related malfunctions.

Brakes should be tested to prove that they render at a load that is equivalent to 60% of the line's MBL. Test results should be recorded.

Brake linings should be renewed if there is any significant deterioration of holding power.

For further information, reference should be made to guidance provided by manufacturers of brake test kits and information contained within *Mooring Equipment Guidelines*.

2.10 Application of Brake

Band brakes are designed to provide their rated holding capacity when tightened to the required torque. With manually-applied brakes, it is difficult to ensure that the required torque is applied as different people are of different builds and can apply different forces to the brake applicator. Figure 12 illustrates the effect of applied torque on brake holding capacity.

Section 2 *Mooring Winches*

Fig. 12 Effect of Applied Torque on Brake Holding Capacity

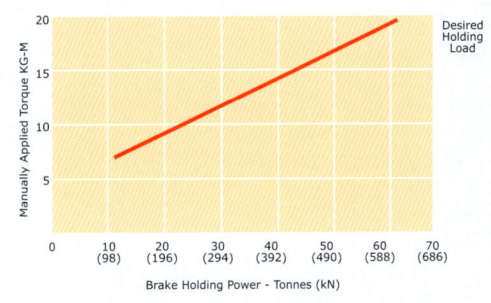

To overcome uncertainties associated with the applied torque, some brake designs include hydraulic actuators or incorporate a spring-applied mechanism with hydraulic or manual release. Whichever brake arrangement is installed, it is important that it is operated properly to achieve the desired holding capacity.

Once a line load is applied to the drum, the band brake will stretch thereby reducing the load on the brake controls. As a result, a manually-applied brake can easily be re-tightened when the mooring line is under high load, even if it was set hard originally. This means that there is no way to determine the proper handwheel torque that is required once the winch is subjected to a high line load. There is a danger that, under worsening environmental conditions, the brake can be re-tightened to a point where the line may part before the brake slips. Caution must, therefore, be exercised when re-tightening brakes to ensure that they are not over-tightened. The problem can be overcome by the use of spring-applied brakes as the spring automatically compensates for the elongation of the brake band assuring a constant holding capacity of the brake.

Effective Mooring

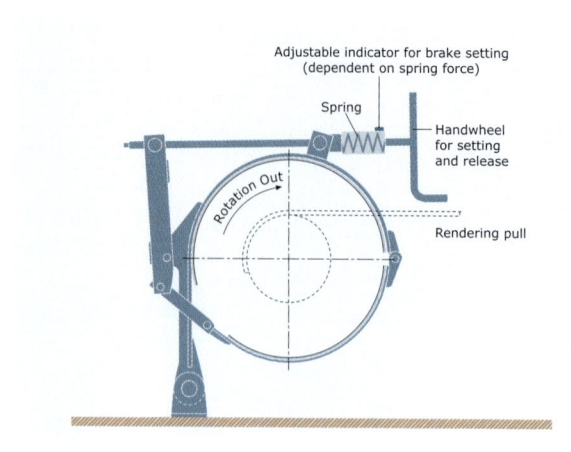

Fig. 13 Spring-Applied Brake with Manual Setting and Release

2.11 Incorrect Use of Brake

The brake is a static device for holding a line tight and it is not intended as a way of controlling a line. If a line has to be slacked down, the winch should be put into gear, the brake opened and the line walked back under power. It should never be slacked down by releasing the brake as this causes increased and uneven wear on the brake band, is uncontrolled and is, therefore, unsafe. Furthermore, if two lines in the same direction have equal loads, the entire load will be suddenly transferred to the other line which may then part.

2.12 Exceptional Circumstances

Occasionally, unanticipated changes of load, perhaps caused by extreme winds, waves, swell or tide, may cause the brakes to slip and the ship to be at risk of moving off the berth. Should this occur, do NOT release the brakes and attempt to heave the ship alongside as this is impossible. Any attempt to do this will only worsen the situation. Tug assistance should be requested, the main engine should be made ready for manoeuvring and

Section 2 *Mooring Winches*

cargo hoses or marine loading arms and gangways should be disconnected.

If the problem is caused by high winds, consideration should be given to reducing the freeboard through the addition of extra ballast where possible.

It should be remembered that the brake holding capacity is always greater than the winch's stall heaving capacity which should never exceed 50% of the mooring line's MBL. Therefore, once the brake starts to render, it is impossible to heave in unless the forces causing the brake rendering are reduced.

Stall heaving capacity, also called stall pull, is the line pull a winch will exert when control is in recover (heave in) and the line is held stationary. Refer to the opening of this section, Section 2.

2.13 Winch in Gear

Winches should never be left in gear with the band brake applied. Hydraulic or electric drives can suffer severe damage should the brake render.

Mooring drums should always be left disconnected from the winch drive whenever the mooring line is tensioned and the band brake is fully applied.

2.14 Freezing Weather

During periods of freezing weather it may be necessary to run steam winches continuously to prevent serious damage to the cylinders, steam pipes, etc. Alternatively, some winches are provided with a steam-to-exhaust by-pass valve that can be adjusted to allow sufficient steam to pass through the system to prevent the pipes from freezing.

Some hydraulic systems also have a warm-up circulating line. Reference should be made to manufacturer's instructions.

Effective Mooring

2.15 Joining a New Ship

It should be obvious that people using the ship's mooring equipment must be trained in its operation and capabilities.

You should not operate any mooring equipment unless trained and authorized by the person in charge. Training should include, where appropriate, the isolation of powered equipment, i.e. turning winches on and off.

Always check the following when joining a new ship:

- Mooring line size, length and type
- type of winch:
  - e.g. self-tensioning, split drum, steam, electric or hydraulic
- heaving power of the mooring winches as %MBL of the attached line
- type of brake mechanism
- brake holding capacity of the mooring winches, as % MBL of the attached line, and to which layer it is applied
- general condition of mooring lines (splices, age, etc.)
- last test date of winch brakes
- that the rope is reeled the correct way round the drum.

"....ensure controls are clearly marked"

Section 2 Mooring Winches

2.16 Safety Reminders

Ensure that the 'heave-in' and 'pay-out' directions are clearly marked on the winch handles and controls.

Ensure that winch drums are marked to indicate correct reeling direction.

Steam pipes in the vicinity of an operator or rope handler must be lagged or adequately guarded against accidental contact.

Do not allow oil leaks from hydraulic winches to go unnoticed. It could be YOU that slips on that pool.

Do not try to assess the tension in a line by kicking or standing on it. This is dangerous and futile.

OCIMF

Effective Mooring,
Your Guide to Mooring Equipment and Operations

Wire Mooring Lines

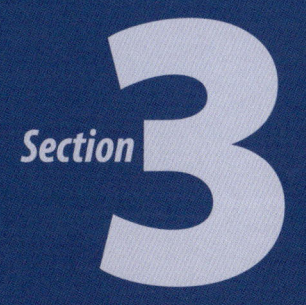

Section 3

Section 3 Wire Mooring Lines

Wire Mooring Lines

3.1 Construction of Wire Mooring Lines

When high minimum breaking load (MBL) together with reasonable ease of handling was required in a mooring line, it was traditional to select steel wire ropes, although the use of alternative high modulus fibre mooring lines, such as HMPE, is becoming more common.

A steel wire rope consists of a number of strands laid up around a central core of fibre or wire. Each strand, in turn, consists of a number of wires laid up to form the strand.

It is normal to describe the rope in terms of the number of strands and number of wires per strand, e.g. 6 x 36, 6 x 41.

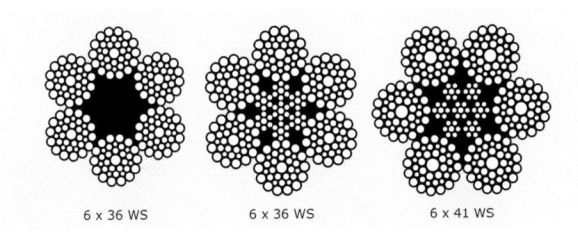

6 x 36 WS   6 x 36 WS   6 x 41 WS

Fig. 14 Strands and Wires per Strand

The first number is the number of strands in the rope. 6 round strands around a central wire or fibre core is the normal construction for marine use. Ropes of 8 strands, or multiple strand design, or triangular strand design are also available, but are normally restricted to specialist applications. The second number is the wires in each strand. Ropes with more wires have greater flexibility and fatigue resistance but less resistance to abrasion. Those with fewer wires have less flexibility and fatigue resistance but more resistance to abrasion. A standard mooring wire is 6 x 36 or 6 x 41 construction.

Effective Mooring

Several constructions are available and the following definitions and illustrations will be of assistance in identifying the different wire types.

3.2 Definitions

Lay

The twisting of strands to form a rope, or wires to form a strand, during its manufacture.

Right-hand or Left-hand Lay

The angle or direction of the strands relative to the centre of a rope.

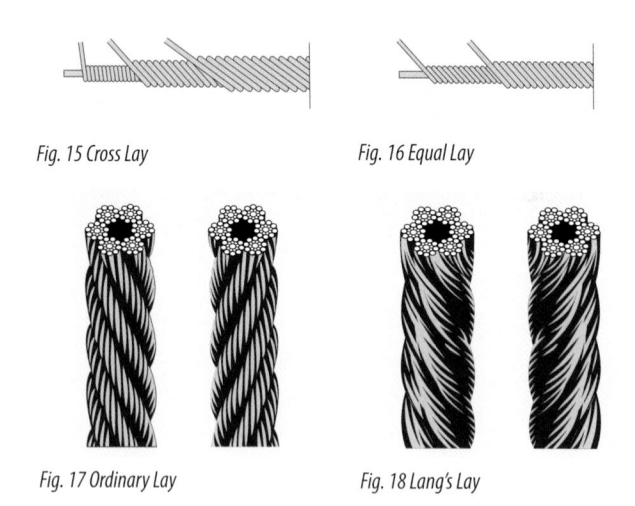

Fig. 15 Cross Lay

Fig. 16 Equal Lay

Fig. 17 Ordinary Lay

Fig. 18 Lang's Lay

Cross Lay and Equal Lay

Terms describing the lay of the wires used to make up the strands. See Figures 15 and 16.

Ordinary Lay

A method of making a rope where the lay of the wires in the strand is opposite to the lay of the strands in the rope. See Figure 17.

Lang's Lay

A method of making a rope where the lay of the wires in the strand is the same as the lay of the strands in the rope. Although this construction has better wearing properties than ordinary lay, because it tends to untwist it has only limited use. It is not used for mooring lines. See Figure 18.

Minimum Breaking Load (MBL)

The minimum breaking load of a new dry mooring line as declared by the manufacturer.

Yield Point

The point at which the ratio of strain/stress increases sharply. This is the point at which a wire may become permanently distorted.

3.3 Typical Steel Wire Rope Constructions

Equal Lay construction gives superior performance over a Cross Lay rope of the same diameter because:

- It possesses a higher MBL. This is because all the layers of wire have the same pitch or length of lay and each wire in each layer lies either in the trough between the wires of the under layer or, alternatively, along the crown of the underlying wire
- no wire crosses over the crown of the underlying wires as in Cross Lay construction reducing internal wear by the elimination of cross cutting.

A standard 6-strand Equal Lay/Ordinary Lay construction is usually adopted for mooring wires. Mooring wires of diameter 22-40 mm are usually 6 x 36 construction and larger wires 6 x 41. Wire ropes can be supplied in right-hand lay or left-hand lay. Unless otherwise specified, a right-hand lay will normally be supplied.

Effective Mooring

Wire ropes can be supplied in different grades of steel. However, a minimum tensile strength of 1,770 N/mm^2 is recommended for pre-formed drawn galvanised wire strands because, for a given diameter of wire rope, an increased MBL and generally better performance is obtained.

Wire ropes can be supplied with fibre cores or steel wire cores. Steel wire ropes with an Independent Wire Rope Core (IWRC) are preferred over fibre core steel wire lines. However, steel wires with fibre cores are easier to handle and may sometimes be found on smaller ships having smaller wire sizes, and where a wire is to be handled manually and 'turned up' on bitts.

Where the wire ropes are used on winch storage drums with little manual handling, it is advantageous to use a steel wire core. Wires constructed using a steel wire core offer a greater resistance to the crushing forces experienced on the storage drums, suffer a smaller loss of MBL when bent, are about 7-8% stronger and extend slightly less (0.25% – 0.5% as opposed to 0.5 – 0.75%) than a fibre core wire rope of the same diameter.

Mooring wires are usually galvanised to provide better resistance to corrosion.

To summarise, the wires most frequently found on self-storing winches will be of the following constructions:

- Equal Lay
- ordinary Lay
- right-hand lay
- independent wire rope core (IWRC)
- usually minimum tensile strength of 1,770 N/mm2
- 6x36 or 6x41.

3.4 Bend Radius

Steel wire ropes will lose strength when bent over a radius. This is a major factor in the design of shipboard equipment such as winch drums and fairleads. A fibre core rope will lose more

Section 3 *Wire Mooring Lines*

strength than an IWRC rope as shown in Figure 19.

As a general rule, a minimum bend radius (D:d) of 12 is recommended. Where this would cause problems with the size of a fitting, a ratio of 10 may be an acceptable compromise for items such as roller fairleads.

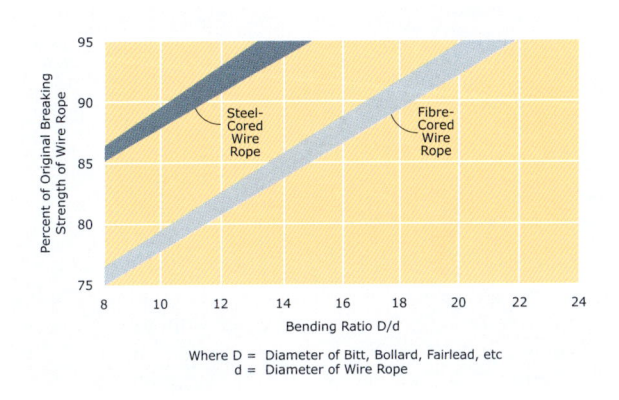

Fig. 19 Effects of Bending on Wire Rope Strength

3.5 Advantages of Steel Wire Ropes

Wire rope is used in preference to conventional synthetic fibre ropes because it possesses:

- Low elasticity, i.e. limited stretch. When a wire is first used under load, there is a slight permanent extension known as 'constructional' stretch resulting from a slight rearrangement of the wires. After this, the wire experiences an elastic stretch that is recoverable and linear up to about 70% MBL; above this, the stretch increases non-linearly until the line breaks
- a strength/diameter ratio superior to conventional synthetic fibre ropes
- a smaller diameter making it suitable for use on winch storage reels.

Effective Mooring

High modulus synthetic fibre ropes, such as those constructed from aramid or HMPE fibres, have elasticity properties and strength/diameter ratios that make them a viable option if considering the replacement of steel wire ropes.

Where synthetic fibre ropes may be used in chocks previously used with wires, those surfaces should be checked that they have not become grooved or roughened. With high modulus fibre ropes, especially, all contact surfaces should be regularly inspected, and kept smooth and free from chafe points. This also applies to winch drums, especially the transfer section between storage and tension drums of split drum winches.

3.6 Certification

When delivered, a certificate should accompany all mooring wires from the manufacturer indicating, among other things, the wire's MBL. These certificates should always be consulted if it is necessary to ascertain the specification of a particular wire.

All wires should be permanently marked so that positive identification with corresponding certificates can be made.

3.7 Stoppers for Use with Steel Wires

There are two methods of stoppering-off a steel wire prior to turning it up on the bitts.

One method is to use a specially designed stopper such as the Carpenter's Stopper (Figure 20). The second and only other recognised method of stopping off wires is to use a length of chain.

Rope must never be used as a stopper on wires because it does not grip the wire well enough.

Section 3 Wire Mooring Lines

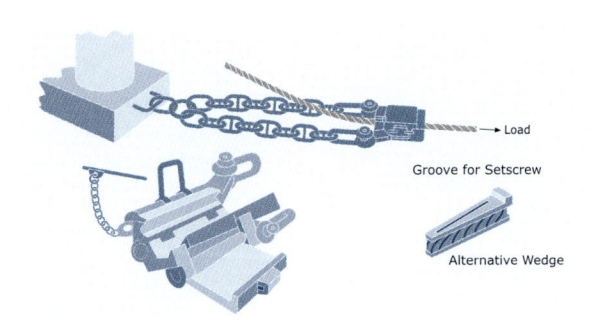

Fig. 20 Carpenter's Stopper

Where a carpenter's stopper is used, it is recommended that the stopper is of equal minimum breaking load to the wire size for which it is designed. An important safety feature of this type of stopper is that, when in position, it is self-tightening and can be left unattended. Further, it will not damage the wire when under load provided it is of correct size and design for the circumference and lay of wire rope on which it is to be used.

Where carpenter's stoppers are not available, a chain stopper should be used taking note of the following:

- When securing a chain stopper to a wire, use only one or two 'Cow Hitches' (also known as 'Lanyard Hitches') (Figure 21), **never** a 'Clove Hitch'
- stoppers exceeding 20 mm diameter are virtually unmanageable and so this is the largest size likely to be encountered
- all chain stoppers should be proof load tested to twice the SWL

Effective Mooring

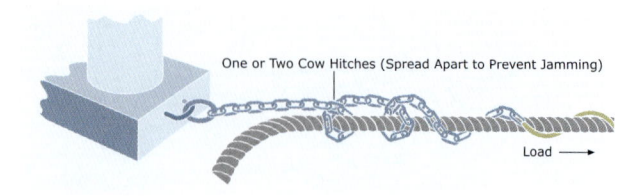

Fig. 21 Chain Stopper

Warning: In most cases the stopper will break at a lower load than the wire.

When ordering the chain stopper, it is important to specify the following:

- Size – diameter of link
- type of chain – close link, higher tensile steel, i.e. tensile strength in the order of 63 kg/mm^2. (Superior grades and higher breaking loads are available if required.)

The following table shows typical breaking loads for Grade 40 steel chain. Note that the diameter is the diameter of the steel forming the link of the chain. The length of chain is usually 3.5-4.5 m.

Chain Size	Typical Breaking Load
12 mm diameter	7.2 tonnes
16 mm diameter	12.7 tonnes
20 mm diameter	19.9 tonnes

Section 3 *Wire Mooring Lines*

3.8 Care of Wire

AVOID **leading wires around sharp edges.**

It damages the wire and seriously reduces the wire's strength.

If a wire is run through a lead that is not aligned with the winch drum, the wire will be damaged where it rubs on the edge of the spool. This practice should be avoided.

AVOID **crossing the wire on the drum.**

This leads to crushing or flattening also seriously reducing the wire's strength.

AVOID **kinking the wire.**

This opens the lay and leaves the wire permanently weakened.

AVOID **leading wires through excessive angles.**

Avoid excessive angles because the wind or current loads, or both, could exceed the wire's MBL on the outboard section of wire (T_2 in Figure 22) breaking the wire before the winch brake renders.

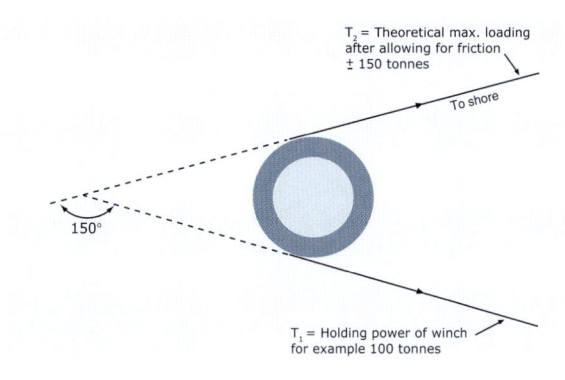

T_2 = Theoretical max. loading after allowing for friction ± 150 tonnes

To shore

150°

T_1 = Holding power of winch for example 100 tonnes

Fig. 22 Friction and Holding Power

43

©Copyright OCIMF 2010

3.9 Maintenance of Steel Wire Mooring Ropes

Steel wire mooring ropes should be lubricated at intervals. However, operators should be aware that many terminals will take exception to any sheen left on the water by the wires following their routine lubrication.

Wire rope deteriorates gradually throughout its entire service life. To keep abreast of deterioration, wire ropes must be periodically inspected. Because moderate degradation is normally present, the mere detection of rope deterioration does not usually justify rope retirement. Operators should establish clear criteria for the discard of wire ropes.

At routine intervals the entire length of rope should be inspected by a competent person with particular attention paid to those sections that are proven by experience to be the main areas of deterioration. Excessive wear, broken wires, distortion and corrosion are the usual signs of deterioration.

To avoid injury to line handlers, broken wires should be removed as they occur by bending them backwards and forwards using a pair of pliers until they break deep in the valley between two outer strands. The number and position of broken wires should be recorded.

The inspection should include ensuring that the ends of the rope are secure. This involves checking the integrity of the anchorage at the drum end and the integrity of the termination at the outboard end. Where eyes are shackled to synthetic tails, regular visual inspection is vital as the shackle tends to increase wear on the wire at this point.

Deterioration of the wire can occur undetected on the bottom layers of the winch particularly when a wire has seen some service and has been turned 'end for end'.

If 'dry' or darkened patches are observed along the wire, the depth and degree of corrosion should be checked. An effective way to do this is to place the wire on a solid surface and strike it with a hammer. This will cause the rust to fall away parting the weakened strands exposing the severity of the corrosion.

Wires should be discarded if the number of visible broken strands is more than 4 over a length of 6d, or 8 over a length of 10d; 'd' being the wire's nominal diameter.

If the nominal diameter of the wire rope is found to have decreased by 10% or more, the rope should be discarded even if no broken wires are visible.

Refer to *Mooring Equipment Guidelines* for further details.

3.10 Selection of Anchor Point for 1st Layer of Wire on a Drum

When fitting a new wire to a mooring winch or replacing an old wire after inspection and lubrication, it is important that the wire is replaced as shown in Figure 23.

Effective Mooring

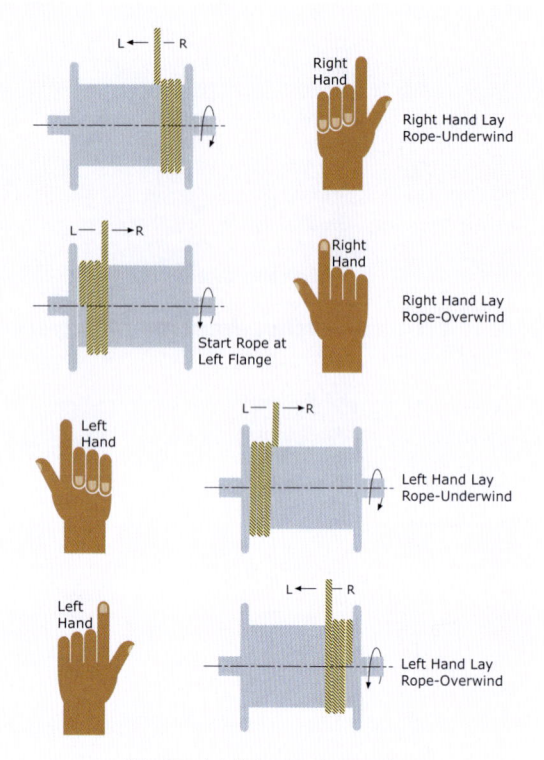

Note: Thumb indicates side of rope anchorage

Fig. 23 Method of Locating Rope Anchorage Point on a Plain Drum

Do not open a new coil of wire without using a turntable or similar apparatus in order to avoid kinking the wire.

Section 3 Wire Mooring Lines

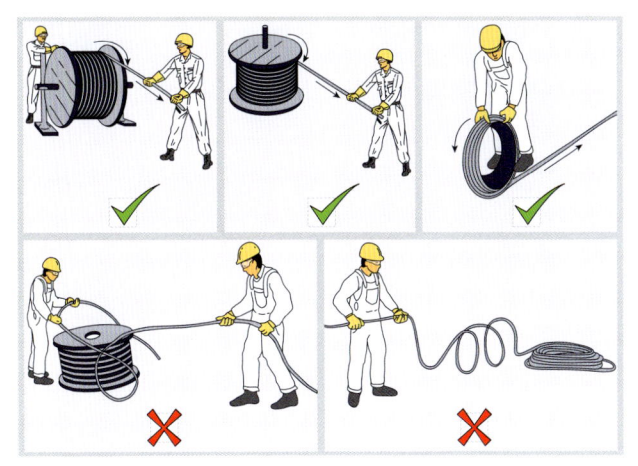

Fig. 24 Uncoiling a New Wire

3.11 Splicing Wire

It is normal practice for mooring wires to be supplied with eyes formed by means of a ferrule applied mechanically by the manufacturer. If the eye is damaged, it can be cut off and a new eye spliced in the wire. Where this is done, there should be a minimum of 5 full tucks and 2 half tucks used. A manual splice, however, will effectively reduce the MBL of the wire by 10-15%. It is preferable to have the eye re-made using a mechanically applied ferrule as soon as practicable. Because it is extremely difficult to put an effective manual splice in a large mooring wire, the practice is not recommended.

Particular attention should be paid to the area around the ferrule during rope inspection. This area is known for developing concentrated corrosion.

Short splices should not be used on wires stored on winch drums as the splice could further deform or damage the wire on the reel.

Effective Mooring

3.12 Safety Reminders

ALWAYS stand well clear of a wire under load.

NEVER stand in the bight of a wire.

ALWAYS wear gloves and other appropriate personal protective equipment when handling wires.

Effective Mooring,
Your Guide to Mooring Equipment and Operations

Synthetic Fibre Ropes

Section **4**

Synthetic Fibre Ropes

4.1 Construction of Synthetic Fibre Ropes

Synthetic fibre ropes are:

- Conventional fibre ropes made from fibres that include polyester, polyamide (previously referred to as 'nylon'), polypropylene, or a mixture of materials
- high modulus synthetic fibre ropes made from fibres that include aramid, high modulus polyethylene (HMPE) and liquid crystal polymer (LCP).

Figure 25 shows the common methods of construction used for synthetic fibre ropes.

Four and six strand with core structures are twisted ropes similar to conventional wire rope and may sometimes be used for mooring lines. They can be relatively stiff in handling, kink if not handled properly and are prone to hockling.

Eight strand ropes, sometimes called square braid or plaited, and twelve strand braided ropes are constructed of left and right-hand laid strands to give a torque-free rope. They are virtually unkinkable, very flexible, easily spliceable and provide a good rope structure for mooring lines.

Double braid ropes, sometimes called braid-on-braid, are constructed of a core braided of many small strands and surrounded by a cover that is also braided of many small strands. The cover provides an integral component to the line's strength. The construction is commonly used for mooring hawsers at single point moorings (SPMs) and for tails on wire ropes.

Parallel strand ropes have the core ropes protected by a non-load bearing protective jacket. They are commonly used for regular mooring ropes and as SPM hawsers.

Effective Mooring

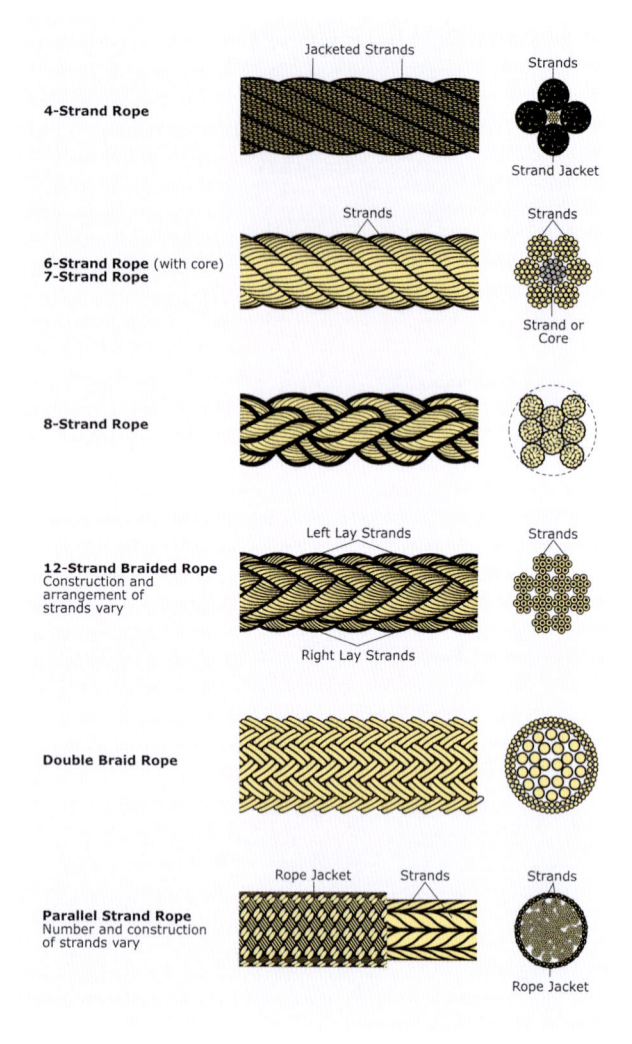

4-Strand Rope	Jacketed Strands	Strands / Strand Jacket
6-Strand Rope (with core) **7-Strand Rope**	Strands	Strands / Strand or Core
8-Strand Rope		
12-Strand Braided Rope Construction and arrangement of strands vary	Left Lay Strands / Right Lay Strands	Strands
Double Braid Rope		
Parallel Strand Rope Number and construction of strands vary	Rope Jacket / Strands	Strands / Rope Jacket

Fig. 25 Construction of Conventional and High Modulus Synthetic Fibre Ropes

4.2 Types of Material Used

The following describes the basic properties of the materials that are commonly used for synthetic fibre ropes.

4.2.1 Conventional materials

Polyester is the most durable of the common materials. It has high strength, both wet and dry. It has good resistance against external abrasion and does not lose strength rapidly due to cyclic loading.

Polyester's low coefficient of friction allows it to slide easily around bitts. Its relatively high melting point reduces the chances of fusion. Polyester is, therefore, useful for large and small ropes where strength and durability are important and where moderate elasticity is required.

Specific Gravity 1.38. Melting Point 256°C.

Polyamide (previously called 'nylon') rope loses 10 – 15% of its strength when wet. It has the highest elasticity of regularly used materials with good temperature and abrasion resistance.

When comparing polyamide with other fibres, or when ordering polyamide lines, it should be noted that it is the dry MBL that is quoted. Due allowance should be made for the strength loss when wet.

Specific Gravity 1.14. Melting Point 218°C.

Polypropylene rope has approximately the same elasticity as polyester rope. Polypropylene has limited temperature resistance and has poor cyclic loading characteristics. Prolonged exposure to the sun's ultraviolet rays can cause polypropylene fibres to disintegrate due to actinic degradation.

Polypropylene is lighter than water and can be used for floating messenger lines. The use of moorings manufactured from 100% polypropylene is not recommended. However, suitable composites or melt mixes with other fibres such as polyethylene or polyester are available and acceptable for use as moorings.

Effective Mooring

Specific Gravity 0.91. Melting Point 165°C.

Examples of combinations of materials include polyamide mono and multifilament fibre mixtures, polyester/polyolefin dual fibre, polypropylene/polyester melt mix, mixed polyolefin. Manufacturers' literature should always be consulted to ascertain the properties and MBL of ropes made from combinations of materials as they will vary greatly depending on the materials used.

4.2.2 High Modulus Synthetic Materials

Aramid fibre typically has high strength and low stretch. It does not creep and does not melt, but chars at high temperatures.

Aramid ropes do not float. They are typically covered (jacketed) with some other synthetic fibre such as polyester to increase abrasion resistance and to protect against UV degradation. Aramid has very good fatigue properties.

Specific Gravity 1.44. Chars at 500°C.

Liquid Crystal Polymer (LCP) fibres have high strength and low stretch. The fibre has a temperature resistance between HMPE and aramid. LCP fibres have excellent long-term durability to fatigue, cutting and abrasion.

Specific Gravity 1.40. Melting Point 300°C.

High Modulus Polyethylene (HMPE) is a fibre with high strength to weight ratio and low stretch characteristics. HMPE fibres have very good fatigue and abrasion properties but limited temperature resistance with a maximum working temperature of 70ºC.

Ropes constructed from 100% HMPE fibres float. However, jacketed HMPE ropes can have a higher density and may sink.

Specific Gravity 0.97. Melting Point 147°C.

High modulus synthetic fibre ropes usually require the use of synthetic fibre rope tails to introduce some elasticity into the mooring system.

Section 4 *Synthetic Fibre Ropes*

4.3 Relative Minimum Breaking Loads of Synthetic Ropes

The following illustrates typical MBLs for a 40 mm rope made from different materials.

Rope Type	MBL
Polyester	24 tonnes
Polyamide	30 tonnes
Poypropylene	21 tonnes
Aramid	110 tonnes
HMPE	124 tonnes

4.4 Certification

When delivered, a certificate from the manufacturer indicating the MBL should accompany all mooring ropes. The certificate should always be consulted if it is necessary to ascertain the specification of a particular rope.

All ropes and tails should be permanently marked so that positive identification with corresponding certificates can be made.

4.5 Stoppers for Use with Synthetic Ropes

Crew members handling synthetic lines which must be stopped off and made fast to bitts need to be properly trained in safe mooring practices. Surging of lines on winch warping drums is not recommended for synthetic lines. The nature of the fibres combined with the high loads make it necessary when providing slack to walk back the winches rather than surging these lines.

With the numerous different types of synthetic fibre ropes available and the great strength of such ropes, it is essential when stopping off these mooring lines that the correct rope stopper is used. Experience has shown that the ideal rope for stoppers should satisfy the following requirements:

- The stopper should be a synthetic fibre rope

Effective Mooring

- the stopper should be used 'on the double'
- the stopper should be very flexible and the size should be appropriate for the size of moorings, i.e. about 50% of the rope's diameter
- the stopper rope should be of low stretch material
- the man-made fibre ropes used for the stopper should be made from high melting point material, i.e. polyester or polyamide
- the double rope used for the stopper should, where possible, have a combined strength equal to 50% of the breaking load of the mooring rope on which it is to be used.

Figure 26 shows the correct method of stopping off a synthetic mooring rope. The stopper may be made fast by a turn around the leading post of the bitts if no ring is available.

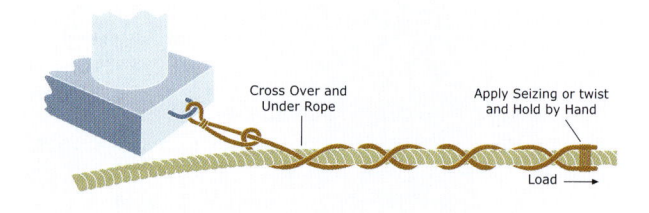

Fig. 26 Stopping Off a Synthetic Fibre Rope

> Conventional synthetic fibre ropes give little or no warning when about to break and possess low resistance to chafing when under load.

4.6 Belaying Synthetic Fibre Ropes on Bitts

When making conventional synthetic fibre ropes fast to bitts, do not use a 'figure-of-eight' alone to turn them up. Use **one full round turn** around the leading post of the bitts before 'figure-of-eighting'. This method allows better control of the rope, is easy to use and is safer.

Section 4 *Synthetic Fibre Ropes*

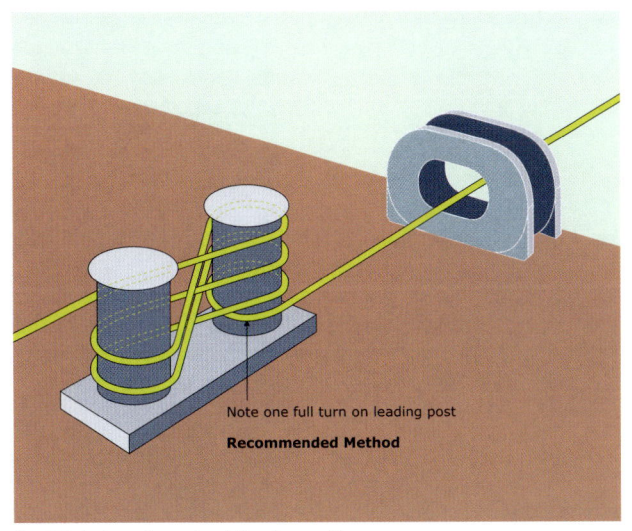

Fig. 27 Belaying a Conventional Fibre Rope on Bitts

Unjacketed high modulus synthetic fibre ropes have a low coefficient of friction and should not normally be handled on warping drums. Should there be a need to belay an unjacketed high modulus line around bitts, for example, when making fast a tug's line, **two full round turns** should be taken around the leading post prior to turning the line up in a 'figure-of-eight' fashion.

4.7 Snap Back

A significant danger when handling mooring lines is 'snap back' which is the sudden release of the energy stored in the tensioned mooring line when it breaks.

When a line is loaded it stretches. Energy is stored in the line in proportion to the load and the stretch. This energy is suddenly released when the line breaks. The ends of the line snap back striking anything in their path with significant force.

The primary rule is to treat every line under load with extreme

Effective Mooring

caution. Stay clear of the potential path of snap back whenever possible! Conventional synthetic lines normally break suddenly and without warning. Unlike wires, they do not give audible signs of pending failure and they may not exhibit any broken elements before completely parting.

This snap back is common to all lines. Even long wire lines under tension can stretch sufficiently to snap back with considerable energy. **Conventional synthetic lines are much more elastic, and so the danger of snap back is more severe**. High modulus synthetic lines have similar breaking characteristics to wire ropes. However, it is noted that snap back from these materials will be along the length of the line and not in a snaking manner, as is found with wire ropes.

Stand well clear of the potential path of snap back (see Figure 28). The potential path of snap back extends to the sides of and far beyond the ends of the tensioned line.

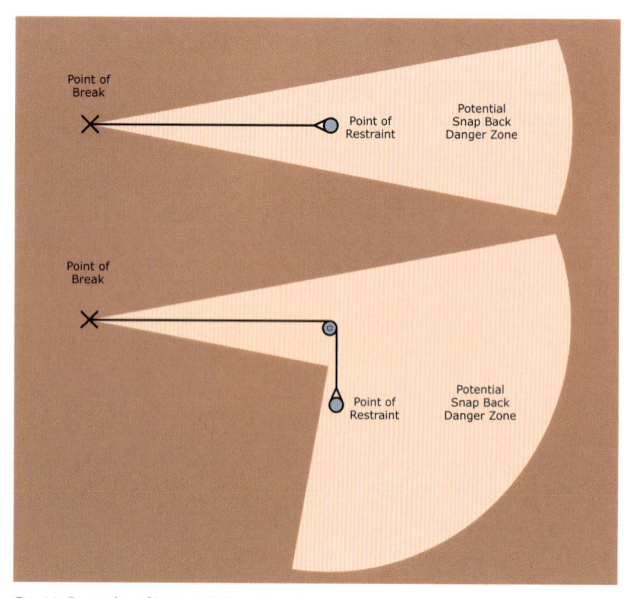

Fig. 28 Examples of Potential Snap-Back Zones

Section 4 Synthetic Fibre Ropes

A broken line will snap back beyond the point at which it is secured, possibly to a distance almost as far as its own length. If the line passes around a fairlead, then its snap back path may not follow the original path of the line. When it breaks behind the fairlead, the end of the line will fly around and beyond the fairlead.

It is not possible to predict all the potential danger zones from snap back. When in doubt, stand aside and well away from any line under tension.

When it is necessary to pass near a line under tension, do so as quickly as possible. If it is a mooring hawser and the ship is moving about, time your passage for the period during which the line is under little or no tension. If possible, do not stand or pass near the line while the line is being tensioned or while the ship is being moved along the pier. If you must work near a line under tension, do so quickly and get out of the danger zone as soon as possible planning your activity before you approach the line.

4.8 Rope Care

- Ropes must be kept clear of chemicals, chemical vapours or other harmful substances. They should not be stored near paint or where they may be exposed to paint or thinner vapours

- ropes should not be exposed to the sun longer than is necessary as ultraviolet light can cause fibres to deteriorate

- ropes should be stowed in a well ventilated compartment on wood gratings to allow maximum air circulation and to encourage drainage

- do not store ropes in the vicinity of boilers or heaters; do not store them against bulkheads or on decks which may reach high temperatures

- ensure that fairleads and warping drums are in good condition and free from rust and paint. Roller heads should be lubricated and freely moving to avoid friction damage to the rope

- do not surge ropes around drum ends or bitts, as the friction temperature generated may be high enough to melt the fibres

Effective Mooring

- if it is necessary to drag ropes along the deck, ensure that they pass clear of sharp edges or rough surfaces
- when using winch stored ropes, do not run them through leads that are not on a direct line from the drum as they are liable to chafe on the edge of the spool
- ensure that winch drums are free of chafing surfaces, especially the transfer section between storage and tension drums of split drum winches.

4.9 Rope Inspection

Ropes must be visually inspected at regular intervals and these inspections should include, as far as possible, inspection of the inner strands.

For synthetic fibre ropes, the amount of strength loss due to abrasion and/or flexing is directly related to the amount of broken fibre in the rope's cross section. Inspections should include looking and feeling along the length of the line to detect abrasion, glossy or glazed areas, inconsistent diameter, discolouration, inconsistencies in texture and stiffness.

Excessive wear in conventional synthetic fibre ropes is indicated by powdering between the strands and results in permanent elongation. This indicates a reduced breaking load and consideration must be given to replacing the rope. If damage is localised, the worn or damaged part can be cut out and the rope spliced.

The inspection should include checking for the security of strands in splices. Generally, a conventional synthetic fibre mooring line should be discarded if it has more than 2 splices within its length.

Refer to *Mooring Equipment Guidelines* for further details.

4.10 Splicing

When a rope is spliced, its breaking load is reduced.

Only trained personnel following maufacturers instructions should splice rope.

Section 4 *Synthetic Fibre Ropes*

High modulus synthetic fibre ropes should, preferably, be spliced ashore as they require specialist splicing.

4.11 Safety Reminders

DO NOT surge synthetic fibre ropes on the drum end; in addition to damaging the rope, as it melts it may stick to the drum or bitts and jump, with a risk of injury to people nearby. ALWAYS walk a winch back to ease the weight off the rope.

DO NOT stand too close to a winch drum or set of bitts when holding and tensioning a line; if the line surges you could be drawn into the drum or bitts before you can safely take another hold or let go. Stand back and grasp the line about one metre from the drum or bitts.

DO NOT apply too many turns over the warping drum end; generally 4 turns should be taken with conventional synthetic lines. If too many are applied then the line cannot be released in a controlled manner.

DO NOT bend the rope excessively.

DO NOT stand in the bight of a rope.

DO NOT stand close to a rope under load, it may part without warning.

DO NOT leave loose objects in the line handling area; if a line breaks it may throw such objects around as it snaps back.

DO NOT have more people than necessary in the vicinity of a line.

Read any government notices, company instructions or 'codes of practice' on board your ship

Effective Mooring

Effective Mooring,
Your Guide to Mooring Equipment and Operations

Offshore Operations

Section 5

Offshore Operations

5.1 Multi-Buoy Moorings

There are two main configurations of Multi-Buoy Moorings (MBMs) commonly found throughout the industry:

- Conventional Buoy Mooring (CBM): an offshore marine berth in which the ship's bow is held in position by its own anchors and a number of mooring buoys, typically 3 to 7, installed to secure the stern
- All Buoy Mooring (ABM): an offshore marine berth in which both the ship's bow and stern are held in position by mooring buoys.

A layout of a typical Conventional Buoy Mooring is shown in Figure 29.

Effective Mooring

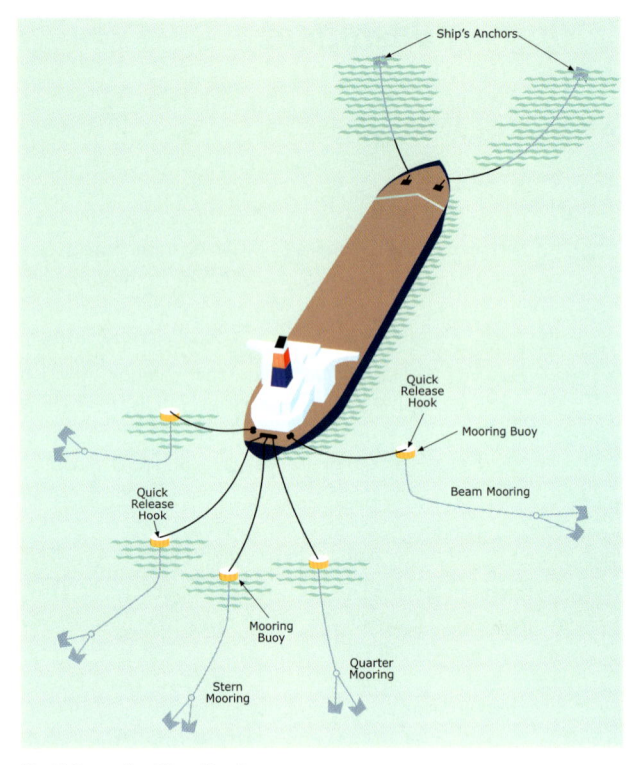

Fig. 29 Conventional Buoy Mooring

The mooring operation is often carried out without tugs requiring the full and efficient use of all the ship's mooring equipment.

The operation starts with the ship carrying out a 'running moor'. While it is most common for the manoeuvre to be started with the stern buoys on the port side of the ship to take advantage of the propeller thrust when the engine is going astern, there are some berths where, for a particular reason, the manoeuvre has to be started with the buoys to starboard. Figure 30 shows the different stages of the operation.

Section 5 *Offshore Operations*

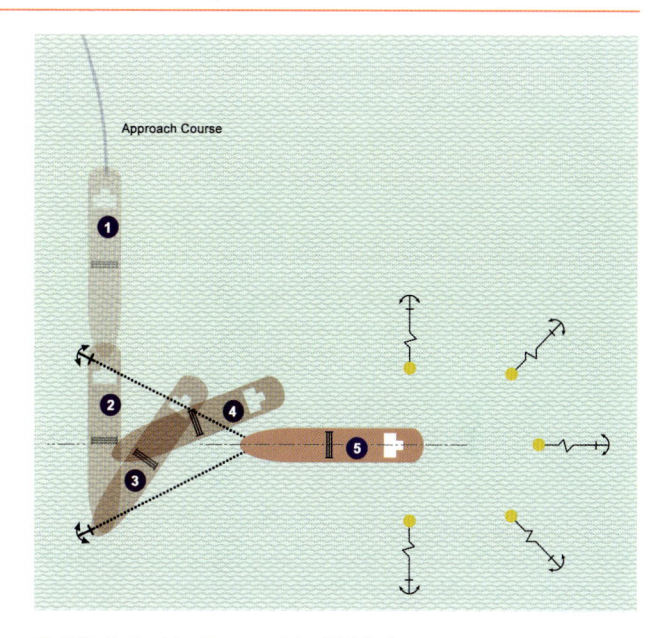

Fig. 30 Typical Berthing Manoeuvre Using Ship's Anchors

The tanker steams slowly towards the forward end of the berth in a line almost perpendicular to her final position. When in the correct position, the starboard anchor is let go and the cable is run out as the ship moves ahead with the engine operating astern. When the ship is stopped in the water, the port anchor is let go. By carefully manoeuvring the engines and helm, and by paying out the port cable while heaving in the starboard cable, the stern of the ship is swung round so that it passes clear of the nearest buoy at the same time as the ship is backing into the sector between the buoys. Mooring lines have to be run to the buoys as quickly as possible to assist in controlling the swing and heaving the ship astern into the berth.

Considerably higher loads than those experienced during a normal berthing operation are imposed on the lines. It is recommended that only lines on drums are used. Because of

Effective Mooring

these higher than normal loads, all the equipment should be thoroughly checked beforehand and only good quality lines should be used. The mooring team should be thoroughly briefed beforehand and be directly supervised by an experienced officer.

At some MBMs, the ship's moorings are supplemented by shore moorings, often wires, run from the buoys or from sub-sea platforms. The handling of heavy wires around the warping drum of a winch and then on to bitts should be done carefully by experienced seamen. When stoppering off the wires prior to securing them to bitts, correctly sized carpenter's stoppers should be used.

During the mooring operation, there are often lengthy periods when mooring boats are operating around the stern and mooring lines are in the water. Good communications between poop and bridge are essential to avoid boats or lines fouling the propeller.

Because the whole operation initially depends on dropping the first anchor in the correct place, leading lines or ranges usually mark the approach line and dropping point. If the anchor is let go too far away, it is virtually impossible to heave the ship into the berth using the moorings alone. The best option is to heave up and start again.

When unberthing and if using shore moorings, they should be stopped off, transferred to the winch drum then walked back using slip wires as necessary. Full-length moorings should never be let go 'on the run' due to the dangerous whipping action of the rope or wire.

The ship's lines are then heaved in as both anchors are weighed and the ship moves forward clear of the buoys. The windward mooring line is usually the last one to be let go to prevent the stern dropping onto the lee buoys.

Section 5 *Offshore Operations*

5.2 *Single Point Moorings*

Fig. 31 Tanker Moored to a Single Point Mooring (SPM)

At a buoy Single Point Mooring (SPM), the tanker bow is secured to the buoy using specially supplied mooring hawsers attached to a swivel on the buoy. This allows the tanker to swing around the buoy in response to wind and tides.

Effective Mooring

Because the ship is only moored at one point, the entire load is borne by the one or two mooring hawsers typically 70-100 m in length. In addition to the normal static loads, considerable dynamic (shock) loads may be experienced as the ship moves to wind, tide and sea. It is, therefore, impracticable for the ship's normal mooring lines to be used. The terminal always supplies the mooring hawsers. These are typically one or two lines each 120-190 mm diameter made from polyamide or polyester with very high minimum breaking loads.

SPM Hawsers - Typical Minimum Breaking Loads		
Diameter	Polyamide	Polyester
120 mm	305 tonnes	219 tonnes
168 mm	570 tonnes	430 tonnes
192 mm	760 tonnes	550 tonnes

With the ship moving significantly while moored to the buoy, the hawsers could quickly chafe on the ship's fairlead. To overcome this, chafe chains are attached to the end of each hawser. It is these chains that pass through the bow fairleads and are connected onboard to specially designed bow chain stoppers (see Figure 32). The chafe chains are composed of 76 mm stud link chain and have typical minimum breaking loads in excess of 500 tonnes.

Fig. 32 Typical Tongue-Type Bow Chain Stopper

Section 5 Offshore Operations

When the berth is unoccupied, the chafe chains are supported by a buoy. A pick-up rope is attached to the ship end of the chafe chain and typically consists of 150 metres of 80 mm diameter (75 tonnes MBL) floating rope complete with an eye at each end. In practice, the rope may vary in length from 120 – 180 metres and in diameter from 64 – 80 mm.

Before the ship commences her approach to the buoy, a messenger line should be made ready running through one of the bow fairleads. This messenger (approximately 24 mm in diameter and of sufficient strength for the operation) should pass through the chain stopper before being led to a winch storage drum. A direct and straight line lead of the pick up rope from the fairlead to the winch storage drum is preferable so that the use of pedestal leads can be avoided, or at least minimised, and the whole operation should be carried out on a 'hands off' basis. The use of winch drum ends (warping ends) to handle pick-up ropes is considered unsafe and should be avoided.

A mooring assistant stationed on the bow normally supervises the mooring operation. He should be accompanied by a responsible officer who is in radio contact with the bridge to pass on the Master's instructions.

To avoid damage to submarine pipelines and SPM anchor chains, the ship's anchor should not be dropped except in an extreme emergency. Most terminals require anchors to be secured during the mooring operation to avoid inadvertent release.

When the ship is close to the SPM, the messenger is lowered to a mooring boat where it will be connected to the pick-up rope. When the boat is clear, this should be heaved on board. The pick-up rope should be heaved in until the chafe chain passes through the fairlead and reaches the required position within the bow stopper. Care should be taken when winching in the pick-up rope and chain to ensure that there is always some slack in the mooring assembly. It can be very dangerous for the mooring crew if the assembly becomes tight before connection is completed. The ship should be carefully manoeuvred to ensure that this does not occur. **The pick-up rope must never be used**

Effective Mooring

to heave the ship into position or to maintain its position.
When the chafe chain is in position, it should be secured in the stopper as quickly as possible.

Once the chain is secured in the stopper, the pick-up rope should be walked back until the weight is transferred to the stopper.

Although tending of moorings is not required, an experienced crew member should be posted forward at all times to observe the moorings and the SPM advising if the tanker starts to ride up to the buoy or starts to yaw excessively.

When unmooring, the weight of the chains should be taken on the winch before lifting the stopper. The chains should then be walked back into the water and the pick up rope slowly paid out through the fairlead.

When mooring to either a CBM or an SPM, always have a few items of essential equipment, such as a large axe, sledgehammer and crow bar, readily available at the mooring station(s).

5.3 Mooring to FPSOs and FSOs

FPSOs (Floating Production, Storage and Offloading units) are generally purpose built or converted tanker hulls anchored in place with oil processing equipment fitted on their decks. They are connected to the oil wells on the sea bed by subsea risers. Internal tanks are used to store oil for export.

FSOs (Floating Storage and Offloading Units) are generally converted tanker hulls that receive processed crude oil from production platforms. They are used to store oil for export.

F(P)SOs use different arrangements for mooring export tankers. The most common systems are tandem mooring arrangements where the export tanker is connected bow-to-stern or bow-to-bow to the F(P)SO using a taut hawser and floating hose arrangement similar to buoy SPMs. Some F(P)SO arrangements utilise a remote buoy SPM. A few use side-by-side offloading, similar to an STS arrangement.

F(P)SOs can be stationed in a number of different ways. From

Section 5 *Offshore Operations*

the point of view of the exporting tanker moored in tandem, the important difference is the ability of the F(P)SO to rotate in azimuth or weathervane. Those that are unable to rotate in azimuth are usually 'spread moored' held in position by a number of anchors. Spread moored F(P)SOs are generally only suited to tandem offloading in benign environmental conditions. Those that rotate in azimuth swivel around an internal turret or external gantry arrangement. Some of these may have the ability to control their own azimuth though thrusters or azimuth pods.

5.4 Dedicated Shuttle Tankers

A number of F(P)SOs operating in harsher conditions are offloaded by dedicated shuttle tankers fitted with specialised bow loading equipment and, in many cases, Dynamic Positioning (DP) systems. DP allows for station keeping astern of the F(P)SO, without putting any tension on the mooring hawser. Non-DP specialised tankers moor directly astern maintaining hawser tension using main engines operating astern at low revolutions or favourable environmental conditions. These vessels generally operate within a smaller weather window than those equipped for DP operations.

Both of the above types of arrangements use specially trained crews familiar with their type of operation and generally receive no assistance from the terminal in mooring and connecting hoses.

Dedicated shuttle tankers will be equipped with Emergency Shut Down (ESD) equipment, linked by telemetry systems to the F(P)SO, for quick release of hose and hawsers. These systems enable the tanker to stop the transfer automatically and release all gear for rapid departure without causing pollution or damaging equipment.

Fig. 33 Typical Tandem Offloading Configuration

5.5 Conventional Tankers

In more benign waters, conventional tankers are used to offload from the F(P)SO. The tanker is moored in a similar manner as at an SPM using one or two mooring hawsers and chafe chain arrangements secured to the ship's bow chain stopper(s).

Floating hose strings are connected to the conventional tanker's midships manifold. They are brought to the ship's side and positioned with the aid of a support vessel then lifted aboard for connection.

A holdback (pull-back) vessel is also often made fast to the stern of the offtake tanker to maintain station at the F(P)SO.

F(P)SOs handling conventional tankers will provide assistance, such as pilots/mooring masters, loading masters and, in some cases, rigging crew for hose connection and disconnection.

All F(P)SO terminals will have specific environmental limits for the safe conduct of operations. These limits should include separate criteria for suspending operations, disconnecting hoses and unmooring.

Section 5 *Offshore Operations*

As noted above, there are a variety of different arrangements for mooring at an F(P)SO. Of particular interest to the export tanker operator are the procedures for approach, mooring, station keeping and offloading.

The differing requirements of these terminals will be detailed in field-specific operations manuals or terminal handbooks which should be provided to vessels using the terminal. Masters should receive notification of the terminal's requirements as part of the pre-arrival information. A briefing should be conducted by terminal representatives before any operation is commenced.

5.6 Mooring Operation

For tandem mooring, the approach is usually made in line with the direction the F(P)SO is lying. Usually, one or more holdback (pull-back) tugs are used to help control the approach by exerting a restraining force at the stern of the export tanker. These vessels are often very powerful multi-purpose field service boats rather than purpose designed ship-handling tugs. Such vessels are not usually suitable for pushing but can be capable of exerting high bollard pull forces on the export tanker well in excess of the SWL of the bitts and fairleads to which the towlines are attached.

- It is recommended that fairleads and bitts, used for tug escort and holdback duties on tankers of 50,000 dwt and above, have a SWL of at least 200 tonnes (at least 100 tonnes for tankers less than 50,000 dwt)

- if the export tanker is not fitted with a special towing strongpoint, it is preferable that the towline is made fast by a 'single eye' on one post of the largest available bitts through a fairlead in the same fore and aft line as close to the centre line as possible. If the towing line has to be turned up, ensure that the first turn is taken around the leading post, as described in Section 4

- towing vessels should be advised of the SWL of the fitting to

Effective Mooring

which the towing line is attached

- it is strongly preferred that holdback tugs provide the complete towing line arrangement terminating at the ship end in a single soft eye. Use of ship's mooring wires on self-stowing drums or removed from drums and turned up is not recommended
- once the towing line is connected, all personnel should stay well clear of the bitts and chocks throughout mooring and loading operations.

5.7 Ship-to-Ship Transfer (STS)

STS transfers of crude oil and petroleum products are performed for a variety of reasons. These include standard operational considerations such as draft limitations of the large vessel and also emergency considerations such as lightening grounded or disabled vessels. When organisers are planning an STS transfer operation, they should ensure that the ships to be used are compatible in design and equipment and that all operations, including mooring, can be conducted safely and efficiently.

An STS transfer operation should be under the advisory control of one individual who is either one of the Masters concerned or an STS superintendent.

One of the two ships, normally the larger, maintains steerageway at slow speed (preferably about 5 knots) keeping a steady course or constant heading. The manoeuvring ship then manoeuvres alongside. It is recommended that the manoeuvring ship approaches and berths with her port side to the starboard side of the constant heading ship. STS transfer operations involving one ship already positioned at anchor are also quite frequent. For such operations, one ship anchors in a pre-determined position using the anchor on the side opposite that which the other ship will moor.

Mooring operations should be managed to ensure safe and efficient mooring line handling. Moorings should be arranged and rigged to allow safe, effective line tending when the ships are secured together. This is particularly true onboard the manoeuvring ship whose mooring lines will normally be used, but should also be addressed on the constant heading ship where rope messengers have to be made ready between fairleads and deck winches. The order of passing mooring lines during mooring and for releasing lines during unmooring should be agreed in advance of each operation.

The mooring plan adopted will depend on the size of each ship and the difference in their sizes, the expected difference in freeboards and displacement, the anticipated sea and weather conditions, the degree of shelter offered by the location and the efficiency of mooring line leads available. Most STS service providers will have a standard mooring plan suitable for the particular location. It is important to ensure moorings allow for ship movement and freeboard changes to avoid over stressing the lines throughout the operation and ensure that they are not so long that they allow unacceptable movement between the ships. Mooring lines leading in the same direction should be of similar material. Lines should only be led through closed fairleads suitable for STS operations. The use of stopper bars to retrofit open chocks is not recommended.

It is normal for the mooring lines to be deployed from the manoeuvring ship. However, when prevailing weather conditions or weather forecasts require it, sending lines from both ships can increase the number of mooring lines. Loads should not be concentrated by passing most of the mooring ropes through the same fairlead or onto the same mooring bitts. Use should be made of all available fairleads and bitts.

A ship's standard complement of mooring lines is generally suitable for STS transfer operations, but ships equipped with steel wire or high modulus synthetic fibre mooring lines should fit soft rope tails to them. The connection between the primary line and the soft rope tail is made with an approved fitting, e.g. Mandel, Tonsberg, Boss shackles or links.

Rope tails should be at least 11 metres long and have a dry breaking strength at least 25% greater than that of the wires to which they are attached in accordance with *Mooring Equipment*

Effective Mooring

Guidelines. Soft rope tails fitted to wire moorings also make it easier to cut mooring lines in an emergency. Long-handled firemen's axes or other suitable cutting equipment should be available at all mooring stations for this purpose.

Strong rope messengers should be readied on both ships. Rope stoppers should be rigged in way of relevant mooring bitts. Where possible, heaving lines and rope messengers should be made of buoyant materials. A minimum of 4 messengers should be provided and ready for immediate use.

Non-pyrotechnic line-throwing equipment may be used to make the first connection. Crews should be advised beforehand and also warned immediately before the equipment is used.

Excessive or uneven tension in mooring lines should be avoided because it can significantly reduce the weather threshold at which the forces in mooring lines will exceed their SWL. Attention should be given to this throughout the STS operation in order to ensure that changes to the relative freeboards do not create excessive strain in the moorings. Studies have demonstrated that peak loads on individual head and stern mooring lines can be minimised if the lead angles are similar. This allows more effective sharing of the mooring loads.

For further information, reference should be made to ICS/OCIMF *Ship-to-Ship Transfer Guide (Petroleum)* and *Ship-to-Ship Transfer Guide (Liquefied Gas)*.

Section 5 Offshore Operations

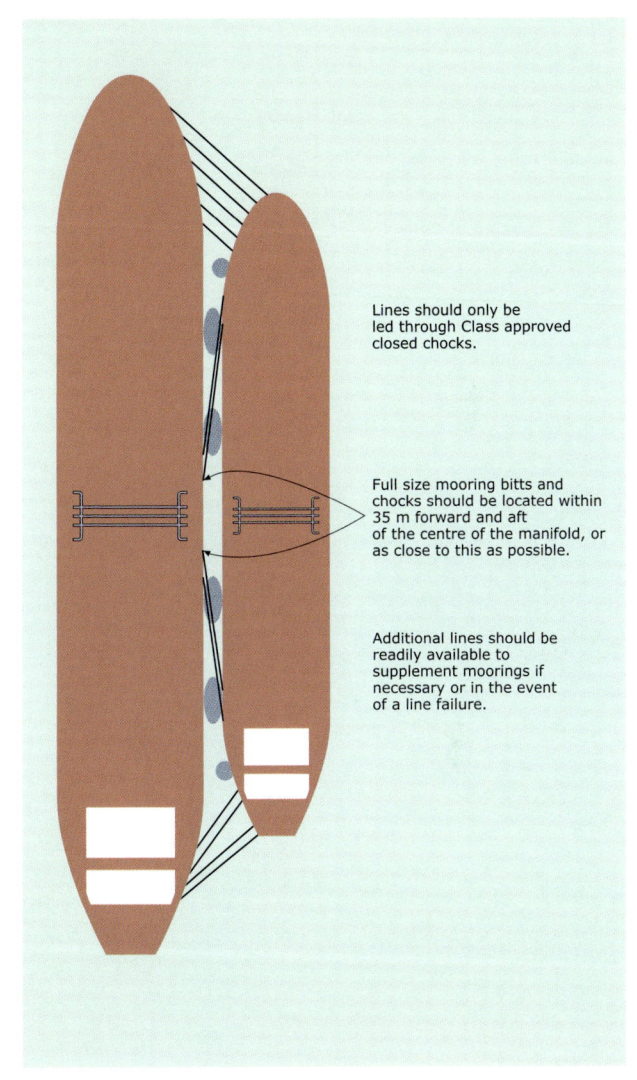

Lines should only be led through Class approved closed chocks.

Full size mooring bitts and chocks should be located within 35 m forward and aft of the centre of the manifold, or as close to this as possible.

Additional lines should be readily available to supplement moorings if necessary or in the event of a line failure.

Fig. 34 Mooring Pattern During Ship-to-Ship Transfer

Effective Mooring,
Your Guide to Mooring Equipment and Operations

Windlasses and Anchoring

Section **6**

Effective Mooring

Section 6 *Windlasses and Anchoring*

Windlasses and Anchoring

It is essential that you read your company's rules and regulations concerning anchoring. They will give clear directions for anchoring procedures. Windlasses are typically designed to lift a maximum weight of an anchor and three free hanging shackles (shots) of cable. Nevertheless, anchor losses sometimes occur on all classes of vessel and have mainly been attributed to:

- Too great a vessel speed over the ground
- too little cable being paid out during the initial lowering of the anchor prior to letting go.

The risk of anchor and cable losses, particularly on large ships such as VLCCs, may be minimised by:

- Ensuring minimum or nil speed over the ground. An indication of speed over the ground can be determined by a number of methods including navigational aids and by observation of the wake while engines are running astern
- the fitting of a speed limiter to the windlass
- in all cases, the anchor should be 'walked' (i.e. lowered with the windlass in gear) out of the hawse pipe until just clear of the water
- anchoring with the windlass in gear. This gives good control over the anchor and cable throughout the operation. It also helps to maintain brake efficiency by reducing wear of the brake lining
- closely monitoring weather and sea conditions when anchored to ensure that the anchor is recovered in good time.

In all cases, care must be taken to avoid over-speeding of the windlass engines to avoid damage and possible catastrophic motor failure. When walking the anchor out by means of the windlass motor, it is important that the vessel's speed over ground is less than the windlass pay-out speed. This is typically 9

Effective Mooring

metres/minute or equivalent to less than 0.3 knots. Higher speeds over the ground may cause the motor to render. Your company should be aware of the risk of overspeeding windlass motors.

6.1 Brakes

Brakes are most effective if tightened up at the moment maximum weight comes on the anchor cable. Further adjustment should then be unnecessary as the changes in load due to changing tides and wind will be borne by the cable stopper.

6.2 Cable Stoppers

Cable stoppers form an integral part of the anchor cable restraining equipment and are designed to take the anchoring loads. Cable stoppers must be used when the vessel is anchored and must be applied only after the brake has been set. This ensures that the brake augments the action of the stopper for additional security.

Fig. 35 Correctly Fitted Cable Stopper

Consideration may also be given to tying down the cable stopper whenever it is in use in order to prevent it jumping when under a heavy load.

Section 6 *Windlasses and Anchoring*

Cable stoppers must also be in position, together with the securing chains, when the anchor is 'home' in the pipe.

6.3 Anchor Cables

It is very important that anchor cable lengths are clearly marked with white paint and, if possible, stainless steel bands even when cable counters are fitted.

It is also advisable to conspicuously paint the second shackle from the bitter end to clearly identify it. This will serve as a visual warning of the approach of the end of the anchor cable.

6.4 Communication

If you are charged with the duty of controlling the anchor during an anchoring operation, be sure that the bridge is aware of precisely what is happening or could happen. The Master is, to a large degree, dependent upon your information. It is important to relay information to the bridge, e.g. the direction and amount of cable paid out with an estimation of whether there is, for example, light, moderate or heavy weight on it.

Before lowering or heaving in the anchor, check over the side for small boats, tugs, etc.

Effective Mooring

6.5 Maintenance of Windlass Brakes

Windlass brakes require careful attention with regard to their adjustment and the greasing of mechanisms.

Where linkages form part of the braking mechanism, it is important that the linkages are **free**.

Malfunction can cause the operator to believe that the brake is fully applied when, in fact, **it is not**.

It is also most important to inspect the tightness of 'bearing keep nuts' and cotter pins, particularly after a refit, where it is known that work has been carried out on the assembly.

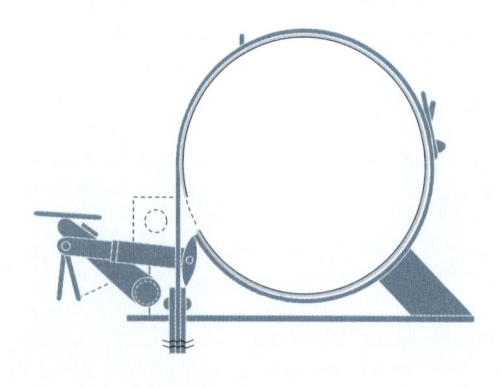

Fig. 36 Typical Brake Arrangement

6.6 Adjustments

Provision is sometimes made to compensate for brake lining wear. Consult the manufacturer's instructions and make sure you are familiar with this feature if provided.

Lack of adjustment for brake lining wear is the most frequent cause of failure in the brake system with subsequent potential loss of anchor and chain.

Section 6 *Windlasses and Anchoring*

If in doubt about the brake holding efficiency – **REPORT IT!**

6.7 Prolonged Periods of Non-Use

After a long sea passage and a port call not requiring the use of either anchor, consideration should be given to a controlled walking-out (i.e. windlass in gear) of the anchors and cable to ensure that the system is still fully operational.

Greasing of bearings, brake linkages, etc. should be carried out during this operation.

6.8 Safety Reminders

> **DO NOT** stand in line with the cable when it is under load or being 'run out' or 'hove in'.
>
> The anchoring party **MUST** wear:
>
> - Safety goggles. The windlass operator should remember that the wearing of safety goggles may reduce his field of vision. Nevertheless, they must be worn
> - safety helmet
> - safety shoes
> - a good pair of overalls with long sleeves.
>
> Flying fragments can injure the operator. Minor injuries could distract him and set the scene for a more serious accident.

Effective Mooring

> Read any government notices, company instructions or 'codes of practice' onboard your ship

OCIMF

Effective Mooring,
Your Guide to Mooring Equipment and Operations

Personal Safety

Section 7

Section 7 *Personal Safety*

Personal Safety

7.1 Handling of Moorings

Remember, you stand a greater risk of injuring yourself or a shipmate during mooring and unmooring operations than at any other time.

Stand clear of all wires and ropes under heavy loads even when not directly involved in their handling.

When paying out wires or ropes, watch that both your own and shipmate's feet are not in the coil or loop.
Beware the bight!

Effective Mooring

Beware the bight!!

Always endeavour to remain in control of the line.

Anticipate and prevent situations arising that may cause a line to run unchecked.

If the line does take charge, **do not** attempt to stop it with your feet or hands as this can result in serious injury.

Ensure that the tail, or bitter, end of the line is secured on board to prevent its complete loss.

When operating a winch or windlass, ensure that you and/or the operator **understand** the controls and **can see** the officer or person in charge for instructions.

Section 7 Personal Safety

DO NOT leave winches and windlasses running unattended. **DO NOT** stand on the machinery itself to get a better view.

DO NOT use a wire directly from a reel that has been designed **only for stowing,** but **do make sure** you have enough wire off the reel **before** you put it into use.

When using a double barrel winch, **ensure that the drum not in use is clear.**

7.2 Safe Handling of Tug Lines

When tugs are used to assist in manoeuvring the ship, additional care is required by the ship's crew.

Effective Mooring

The condition of the tug's lines is unknown and the crew on mooring stations will not normally be aware of when the tug is actually heaving or what load is being applied to the line.

It is, therefore, important to stay well clear of the towline at all times. Beware the snap-back zone!

When the tug is being secured or let go, the person in charge of the mooring should monitor the operation closely to ensure that no load comes onto the line before it is properly secured or while it is being let go.

Never let a tug go until instructed to do so from the bridge. Do not merely respond to directions from the tug's crew.

If the towline has an eye on it, heave this past the bitts so that there is sufficient slack line to work with, stopper-off the line, then put the eye on the bitts. Do not try to manhandle a line on to the bitts if there is insufficient slack line. If the line has no eye and is to be turned up on the bitts it should always be stoppered-off before handling it.

Section 7 *Personal Safety*

Do not try to hold a line in position by standing on it just because it is slack, if the tug moves away so will you.

When letting go, do not simply throw the line off the bitts and let it run out. Always slack the line back to the fairlead in a controlled manner using a messenger line, if necessary, to avoid whiplash.

7.3 Gloves

Gloves protect the hands against abrasion and also provide insulation against very hot or cold conditions, both of which could affect a person's handling of equipment.

Wire should not be handled without leather or similar heavy protective gloves. These can prevent wounds caused by 'snags' (broken wire strands). Such wounds may become infected leading to further medical complications.

Loose fitting gloves are more liable to become trapped between wires and other equipment, such as drum ends or bollards, and do not provide the necessary degree of protection.

Effective Mooring

It must always be remembered that gloves cannot be relied upon to provide complete protection against snags in the wire. Also, snags may catch in the glove material and endanger life and limb through trapping. Such an event can be prevented by attention to the practices described earlier in Section 3 where any snags are dealt with as soon as they are found. Purpose designed steel hooks may be used to minimize physical contact when handling mooring wires.

7.4 Safety Reminders

DO NOT attempt to handle a wire or rope on a drum end **unless** a second person is available to remove or feed the slack rope to you. Someone should also be able to stop the winch immediately in the event of a problem.

DO NOT work too close to the drum when handling wires and ropes. The wire or rope could 'jump' and trap your hand.

ALWAYS wear safety helmets with chinstraps properly tightened during mooring operations.

Gear wheels and other moving parts must be protectively covered. If any guards are missing:

- **Report it!!**
- have them replaced as soon as possible.

Keep your distance.

Section 7 Personal Safety